THE
PARENT'S
PROBLEM
SOLVER

Smart Solutions for Everyday

Discipline Dilemmas and

Behavioral Problems

CATHRYN TOBIN, M.D.

THREE RIVERS PRESS • NEW YORK

Author's note: The anecdotes included in this book are based on stories and experiences parents and friends have shared with me over the years. The individuals' names and personal characteristics have been changed to protect their privacy.

Published by Three Rivers Press, New York, New York.

Member of the Crown Publishing Group, a division of Random House, Inc.

www.randomhouse.com

THREE RIVERS PRESS and the Tugboat design are registered trademarks of Random House, Inc.

Printed in the United States of America

Design by Lindgren/Fuller Book Design

Library of Congress Cataloging-in-Publication Data

Tobin, Cathryn.
   The parent's problem solver: smart solutions for everyday discipline dilemmas and behavioral problems/Cathryn Tobin.—1st ed.
   1. Discipline of children.   2. Parent and child.   3. Child rearing.   I. Title: Smart solutions for everyday discipline dilemmas and behavioral problems. II. Title.
HQ770.4 .T6 2002
649'.64—dc21

2002018135

ISBN 0-609-80761-7

10 9 8 7 6 5 4 3 2 1

First Edition

To my loving parents, Rose and Sidney Tobin,
who taught me the importance of making a contribution
to society and, with their deep love, encouraged
me to believe in myself.

*In loving memory of my father, Dr. Sidney M. Tobin,
my hero—and a truly fine parent and person.*

ACKNOWLEDGMENTS

I thought it would be easy to write a parenting book! After all, I'm an expert in the field. Never in my wildest dreams did I imagine that it would take the support, commitment, and collaboration of so many players. I am grateful to many people for their time, ideas, guidance, baby-sitting services, feedback, patience, understanding, and encouragement.

This book would not have come into being were it not for the untiring support of my husband, Henry. Juggling his demanding career, committees, obligations, and aspirations while keeping the family on track could not have been easy. Thanks for your generosity of time and spirit. You are a true partner and friend.

Next are my children: Benjamin, Marissa, Max, and Madison. They are my inspiration. Whether we're playing Foosball, baking bread, watching a movie, or just hanging out, my favorite moments are the ones we spend together.

I am deeply grateful to my mother and father for the love and encouragement that I've known my whole life. To my mother, I thank you for teaching me about what's important in life. You are a truly wonderful parent and friend.

I could not have asked for a more supportive agent, Tanya McKinnon, who devoted an enormous amount of time and energy helping me launch this project. I am lucky. Without her dedication and perseverance, I would not have been able to successfully carry this book to term.

I'd like to thank Becky Cabaza, my editor at Three Rivers Press, for her creative guidance, expertise, and foresight. She took my random thoughts and shaped them into a design that would benefit others. I am deeply grateful for her humanity, vision, and critical thinking. Without her wisdom, this book would not have been possible.

I would like to offer my sincere gratitude to my sisters, Victoria and Debrah: Victoria for her creative inspiration, and Debrah, my traveling buddy, who accompanied me to Maui and New York so I could attend writer's conferences. And I appreciate my sister-in-law, Guela, who despite a hectic schedule found time to review my writing.

Last, to the parents in my practice who shared their experiences and stories, I extend my personal gratitude.

CONTENTS

FROM A TO Z

Contents

INTRODUCTION

Wouldn't it be great if you had a pediatrician for a best friend? You could turn to her any time of the day or night, and you wouldn't need to wait three weeks for an appointment to see her. Wouldn't it be amazing if your pediatrician friend loved to talk about your problems? She wouldn't criticize, lecture, or judge you. What if your pediatrician friend were also a midwife? Wouldn't that be quite something? She'd respect the practical, holistic, and scientific viewpoints. And if she were also a mother, she'd know you in ways that only another soccer mom, working mom, chauffeur mom, previously stay-at-home mom, and onetime single mom could.

On the surface, those are the particulars of my life. But on a deeper note, I'd like to share with you a few personal experiences that will explain my passion for writing this book and help you to understand why I care more about family life than anything else in this world—as I suspect you do, too.

In 1976, a few days before my twenty-first birthday, my heart was broken, but not by puppy love or failed grades. My son, Aaron, died of a heart defect on his third day of life. I should have been breast-feeding and changing my new baby's diapers, but instead I sat paralyzed with my inescapable loss. For months I sat on the couch, the room filled with my sadness and no one there to break my silence.

As part of the healing process, I began training as a lay midwife in Vancouver, British Columbia. Midwifery was considered illegal at the time, but the pull was so strong that I trained anyway. Initially, I attended home births as an apprentice and learned the art of midwifery from hands-on experience. Years later, with my second (and thankfully, healthy) child and husband in tow, I moved to El Paso, Texas, to get formal training. Wanting to learn the art of midwifery, and fully expecting births to be gentle and nurturing, I discovered instead the reality of how unkind deliveries are when complications arise without a hospital or experienced help nearby. Although I became a licensed midwife and attended more than four hundred home births (and was grateful for the experience), I eventually realized that midwifery was not for me.

When I began medical school, I fully intended to become an obstetrician, but after my first rotation in the neonatal intensive-care unit, where I was drawn like a magnet to the incubators barely filled by the babies inside, I shifted gears and chose pediatrics instead. I've been rewarded by this decision ever since.

Fast-forward twenty years: My private pediatric practice has grown by leaps and bounds. And I'm now the mother of four lovely kids of my own—Benjamin, Marissa, Max, and Madison. I didn't plan to specialize in solving parenting problems, daily, ordinary, highly complicated, or otherwise. But after focusing on family issues for my entire adult life, I have learned what works and what doesn't even come close. It all started back in 1977, when I was a labor coach and prenatal instructor for new mothers and fathers demanding greater control over their birthing experience. Back then, the concept of patients' rights was a radical one. Acting as a go-between on the parents' behalf, I stayed with mothers from the first contraction until the baby was safely at home. Very eighties, but, going nowhere, I decided to get formal training. During my stint in midwifery, where the benefits of modern medicine were not readily available, I learned to interpret a baby's needs in part by paying close attention to his or her cry, body language, and facial expressions—a skill that has proven invaluable to me later in life.

Next I trained as a medical doctor and pediatrician. I learned about normal development and childhood illnesses, cared for youngsters with serious disorders, and provided support and information to families. Before long, I realized that my expertise in "reading" a baby's behavior was not limited to newborns. I found myself interpreting the child's perception of parent-child conflicts, and with this information I was able to clarify for moms and dads why their conventional discipline methods weren't working. Suddenly, parents understood why they were still struggling with their kids. Now, after successfully helping literally tens of thousands of families fix problems such as potty training, picky eating, sleeping hassles, bickering, not listening, and tantrums, I have written this book to help you. I have a great deal to say and many ideas to share that will allow you to manage the emotionally charged and physically exhausting challenges of raising kids in today's frenzied and sometimes mother-unfriendly world.

My goal in writing this book is to help you break free from ineffective styles of managing problems, and to provide you with the tools and philosophies necessary to think and behave in new ways. My plan is to provide you with the skills and information you need to understand and solve your problems and, in doing so, help you become a more confident and effective parent. After working with families for twenty-odd years, I have come to see that each mother and father is truly a loving, capable, and thinking person who, in the act of guiding a child, can discover his or her finest self.

THE
PARENT'S
PROBLEM
SOLVER

THE NEW FLAVOR
OF DISCIPLINE

Twenty years ago, a sixty-pound redheaded dynamo by the name of Sam charged into my office and made me rethink everything I'd learned about discipline during my pediatric training. He was a typical high-energy seven-year-old boy—only he hated school and refused to behave no matter what kind (or amount) of discipline or guidance I recommended to his parents. Like many other parents, Sam's mother and father wondered if they were doing something wrong. If Sam's rebelliousness was at all tied in to how they were handling things, then more than anything else in the world, they wanted to fix their mistakes.

And here were Sam's parents, sitting in my office waiting for me to explain why no amount of threats or bribes, yelling, negative reinforcement, limits, time-ins or time-outs, consistency, "good" communication, or learning from consequences was making one bit of difference. If anything, the attempts to reshape Sam's behavior were sending him into a wild tailspin. Indeed, all the textbook instructions, the same ones my colleagues and I had been dispensing for more than a decade, were only making things worse.

As Sam's parents were telling me about all the trouble that he had gotten himself into during the past week, I was struck by a depressing notion. If Sam's downward cycle of misbehavior continued, in five years' time this enthusiastic and creative youngster would likely become a sullen, resentful, and angry teenager. Although I'm embarrassed to admit it, when my advice hadn't worked in the past, I'd blame the parents, the teachers, society, television, or the electronic age. But as I organized my thoughts that day, I told myself "If Sam's parents are following my advice and my advice isn't working, then maybe something is fundamentally wrong with the advice."

That realization marked the turning point in my thinking. If I was going to be able to truly help Sam and his family, then I would need to go back to square one and reevaluate all my textbook answers. And that's how I discovered something truly amazing, something that changed how I approached behavioral problems in my office and home life forever. To put it bluntly, I realized that parents unintentionally perceive their kids as responsible for the problems encountered in their upbringing, while in reality, adults and children create their dynamics and issues together.

Indeed, when we have trouble in our adult relationships, we are told to "get real" about our contribution to problems. But when it comes to parenting, we often completely forget the concept of reciprocity and readily blame our kids while sparing ourselves criticism (let alone responsibility). For instance, take whining: a strategy that a child uses to influence his parents. For whining to be effective, there must be a *whiner* on one end of the equation and a *parent who caves in* on the other. Together, parent and child *do* whining, with the behavior of each an essential part of the interactions between them.

By becoming more aware of the workings of parent-child relationships, we can learn to manage our problems by *changing our behavior* rather than by trying to *change our kids*. To put it another way, if there is something about a child's habits or behavior that needs changing, the first question that needs asking is "Is this something I need to work on in myself?"

Now, don't get me wrong; I'm not claiming that you'll never need to reprimand your kids again. I'm sure there will still be times when it's needed. But what I am saying is this: These philosophies and practical skills will help you become a more insightful parent and allow you to respond to conflicts with greater self-control and confidence. They will also maximize your chance of solving problems in a fraction of the time, without strong-arm tactics.

Loving and caring for your child when he's* behaving like a little angel is easy and fun. But the true challenge, and what separates good parents from *really* great parents, is the ability to solve problems, ordinary and unexpected, in a way that will protect a child's core self and provide him with a strong and loving base from which to go out into the world.

*For the purpose of simplicity, I will interchange the pronouns "he" and "she" when talking about children.

THE THREE R'S
Reframe, Reflect, Resolve

Most of us think of the three R's as reading, writing, and arithmetic, the essential components to the education and intellectual growth of our children. However, equally essential are the three R's that help parents examine their own behavior. This three-step strategy will allow you to negotiate your way through almost any situation, controlling your knee-jerk reactions and choosing a way of responding to difficulties that will encourage a new reaction from your child. Each of the three steps is an effective tool on its own, but linked together, they form a powerful vehicle for working your way through problems.

The Three R's. The following questions are not intended to make you feel guilty about your past behavior. Rather, they're designed to help you understand the patterns in your actions, perceptions, or thinking that need to change in order for you to become a more effective and nurturing parent. In my experience, parents who write down their answers are more likely to make significant and lasting changes.

Reframe. Reframing means zeroing in on *you* and discovering how you're caught up in the problems that cause you grief. The best way to reframe your problems is to stop looking outside of yourself for answers. Learn to ask *effective* questions about whatever's troubling you. Here's an example of an ineffective question: "Why does my baby need me to rock him to sleep every night?" A more powerful question is "Why have I been rocking my baby to sleep for the last nine months?" Do you see the difference? Effective questions are the ones that lead you to think about yourself, your emotions, your thoughts, and your behavior. When you ask questions that focus on you, they lead to answers that you can do something about. This shift in your thinking may seem minuscule, but the positive impact on your child is enormous.

For example:

- Instead of a less effective question like: Why won't my kids stop fighting?
- *How am I contributing to problems of sibling rivalry?*
- Instead of: Why is my son such a slob?
- *How can I help my son become more organized?*
- Instead of: Why won't my child stop whining?
- *How am I encouraging whining?*
- Instead of: Why is my child such a liar?
- *Is the way I discipline my child encouraging him to lie to me?*
- Instead of: Why won't my daughter stay in her own bed?
- *How do I contribute to my child's sleep problems?*

Reflect. In the first step, you acknowledged that you're tangled in the situations that frustrate you. Now let's discover *how.* This doesn't mean you have to probe your past or get in touch with your feelings. It means you have to make clear observations about parent-child dynamics and use this information as a starting point to bring about change. Discover how you *do* the problem. Zoom in and focus on you. Notice your behaviors, feelings, perceptions, even your body language and facial expressions. For now you don't need to understand the motivation or explanation behind why you do what you do; just become more aware of how you're helping to shape the problem. Become a photojournalist studying you. I've put together an acronym to help you think about the ways in which your behavior, thoughts, and feelings are unwittingly contributing to the problem at hand: S-T-O-P.

See. Replay the situation that is causing you grief. You should be able to visualize the scene in minute detail.

Think. How does your thinking influence the way you respond? For example, let's say you're having trouble getting your six-year-old daughter off to school each morning. You might be thinking, "My child *should* be able to get dressed and ready for school without me walking her through each step." This thought may stop you from trying different ways of dealing with the situation; instead you do more of the same, and the problem escalates without any forward movement.

Observe. Take a step backward and notice your body language, tone of voice, and facial expressions. Imagine you're a photographer who has captured the moment on film. What do these photos illustrate that helps you better understand the problem?

Put it together. Understand the interwoven emotional and mental factors that shape the problem. For example, you may rush into your baby's bedroom and swoop him out of his crib the moment he cries. The reason you do this is that you feel guilty, and you feel guilty because you equate letting your baby cry with negligence. The more aware you are of your perceptions and emotions, the easier it is to put an end to ineffective patterns of behavior.

> ## THE FIFTY-FIFTY FORMULA
> *You and your child each contribute equally to the child-rearing problems that are causing you grief.*

Resolve. Get ready to solve your problems. To break ineffective cycles of behavior, you need to: 1) recognize that you're

THE RULE OF EIGHT

On average, it takes at least eight separate "lessons" where you respond to your child's actions in a new way before he/she will show any signs of changing. In fact, things may actually get worse before they get better. But success will come if you persevere.

"stuck"; 2) get real about your contribution to the problem; 3) make a conscious effort to change; 4) make changes that respect your child as a thinking and feeling individual; and 5) have confidence in your youngster's ability to change.

In the following chapters, we are going to use our three R's method to analyze specific problems, and you'll use this information to move forward. If thousands of frustrated parents whom I've helped over the years could become more confident about their parenting abilities by using the strategies I lay out in this book, then you can, too!

HOW TO LEARN
FROM THIS BOOK
Using the Three R's

Whether your problems are big or small, old or new, I am going to help you solve them by showing you how to *respond* rather than *react* to difficulties. When we react to a problem, we inadvertently reinforce or strengthen it; when we respond, we act in a manner that brings about change. I call this process taking "response-ability," or in other words, developing the ability to respond to a problem in a manner that resolves it.

I've organized this book to be practical. Topics are arranged in alphabetical order, and information is presented in easily handled chunks that can be put into action right away. It is designed to be a source of information, support, and guidance by leading you through a process of analyzing, strategizing, and action. At the end of each chapter, I will ask you to pause and think through your unique situation using the three R's. The act of becoming more conscious, of standing back and choosing how to act—rather than acting on impulse—allows you to guide and direct your children wisely. You have the ability to do this, and nothing is more meaningful, worthwhile, or precious.

How to Use the Three R's to Solve (Just About) Any Parenting Problem

I'd like to show you how to size up a problem—big or small—and make an on-the-spot, in-the-moment adjustment that will ease whatever situation is troubling you. Most often the solution is straightforward and involves a combination of common sense, compassion, and perseverance. Although I cannot be there to help you analyze and strategize around your personal situations, the philosophies and skills you discover in this book will allow you to do this on your own. Remember to be guided by a solid trust in your child and steadfast confidence in yourself. And above all, relish the difficulties and conflicts you encounter, even the most nerve-racking ones, as each one provides a valuable opportunity to love and guide your child.

The Problem

"My spouse and I disagree on how to discipline our toddler. I come out being the heavy because he/she hates to see his/her 'little princess' upset."

Reframe It

Ask yourself, "How am I reacting to our differences?"

Reflect on It

Do I take a tougher stand to compensate? What is the impact of our different approaches? Is my child learning to take advantage of this gap? How have I tried to resolve things? Are there other issues here?

Resolve It!

Try and understand where your partner is coming from. Make it a priority to work on your problems rather than choosing to stay angry. Be clear what it is you're disagreeing about.

•   •   •

The Problem

"My mother in-law criticizes everything I do with my kids."

Reframe It

Ask yourself, "How am I giving her permission to criticize me?"

Reflect on It

What do I say or do when my in-law comments on my parenting? What message is that sending her? How can I respond in a way that tells her to stop interfering while keeping the peace?

Resolve It!

Make mutual respect a priority. Learn to respond to unwelcome advice in a way that puts an end to it. For example, say, "I know you mean well, but I would appreciate support instead of criticism."

•   •   •

The Problem

"My son is stubborn. Sometimes I let him do what he wants because I don't have the energy to fight."

Reframe It

Ask, "How am I enabling his stubbornness?"

Reflect on It

What am I doing to give him the impression that he doesn't need to listen to me?

Resolve It!

Focus on setting limits (see "Listening," page 150). Your child may have an inflexible temperament and need warning about upcoming changes.

.   .   .

The Problem

"My kids fight the moment they get in the car."

Reframe It

Ask yourself, "What am I doing about the car fights?"

Reflect on It

What am I doing to prevent car fights? How do I deal with them when they happen?

Resolve It!

Stop responding in the same way while hoping for a different outcome. Use forward thinking and plan ways to stop the fighting before it happens.

.   .   .

The Problem

"My baby refuses to let anyone hold her except me."

Reframe It

Ask, "How am I responding to my baby's clinginess?"

Reflect on It

Am I interpreting this as a sign of insecurity? Do I force the baby to go to others? Do I try and sneak out?

Resolve It!

Separation anxiety is a normal developmental milestone. Be reassured that your child is developing normally and loves you very much.

• • •

The Problem

"My kids watch too much television."

Reframe It

Ask, "Why do I allow my kids to watch so much television?"

Reflect on It

Have I established clear television rules? Do I enforce them?

Resolve It!

Set clear, nonnegotiable television rules.

• • •

The Problem

"My kids refuse to do their chores."

Reframe It

Ask yourself, "How is my behavior connected to chores not getting done?"

Reflect on It

Do I help my kids get started? Am I providing enough guidance? Do I give too many chores?

Resolve It!

Set a time for chores to be done. Help your kids get started. Praise them for their efforts. Don't criticize the job they've done.

. . .

The Problem

"My daughter refuses to get dressed in the morning."

Reframe It

Ask yourself, "Am I approaching the problem in a way that's helping things?"

Reflect on It

Do I get into battles that could be avoided? Am I allowing enough time to get ready? Are my expectations realistic given what I know about my child's temperament? What am I doing to solve the problem proactively?

Resolve It!

Get up fifteen minutes earlier to avoid feeling rushed. Try different strategies. Ask your child what would help her with her morning problems. Make a poster of what you expect her to do each morning.

. . .

The Problem

"My toddler resists taking a bath."

Reframe It

Ask, "How am I influencing my child's bath-time shenanigans?"

Reflect on It

Am I helping or hurting things? What's wrong with a sponge bath, anyway? Am I getting into unnecessary power struggles?

Resolve It!

Fears are a normal part of childhood. Use sponge baths for now. Talk to your child to reassure him. Say, "I know you're not keen on having baths, but I know you'll enjoy them later."

. . .

The Problem

"All of my friends' children are toilet trained, and mine isn't."

Reframe It

Ask, "What am I really worried about?"

Reflect on It

Am I in competition with my friends? Do I feel like their kids are smarter or better than mine? Am I worrying about what my friends are saying or thinking behind my back?

Resolve It!

Refuse to compete. Toilet training will be easier if your child isn't under pressure. Drop out of the hyperparenting mindset, and appreciate your child for who he is, not what he does.

·   ·   ·

The Problem

"My baby was sleeping through the night before our trip to Maui. Now he's up every hour."

Reframe It

Ask yourself, "How can I encourage my child to sleep through the night—again?"

Reflect on It

Have I reconditioned my child to need me to fall asleep? Am I directing or reacting? Have I been waiting for him to change instead of taking the lead?

Resolve It!

Parents need to direct their kids to establish proper sleep routines, not once but many times. Expect vacations and illness to set you back.

· · ·

The Problem

"My four-year-old can't sit still."

Reframe It

Ask, "How am I responding to her naturally high energy level?"

Reflect on It

Am I asking for the impossible at this time? Am I confusing a trait with a bad habit? How can I get her to focus without hurting her spirit? Am I assigning blame to something that isn't her fault?

Resolve It!

Understanding and accepting your child's temperament is the greatest gift you can give her, and the first step toward bringing out the best in her.

· · ·

The Problem

"My eighteen-month-old still gets up at least twice each night. We live with my in-laws, who feel it's cruel to let her cry, but it's me who gets up with her, and I'm wiped!"

Reframe It

Ask yourself, "What am I doing to resolve this oh-so-sticky situation?"

Reflect on It

Am I considering any strategies or solutions to remedy the problem? Am I discussing the situation with my partner or in-laws?

Resolve It!

Living with in-laws can be tricky when there is a difference of opinion around child-rearing issues. Consider directing your child toward better sleep habits during a holiday or when the grandparents are away. You'll come up with a remedy if you look for one.

ASSESS YOUR PARENTING PROBLEM-SOLVING STYLE
You Can't Change What You Don't Know

Understanding your parenting style is the first step to changing it in order to become a more effective and confident parent. Although you may not realize it, the way you respond and interact with your children forms a consistent pattern of behavior known as your parenting style. There are basically four styles of parenting: *authoritative, permissive, accidental,* and *mindful.* The following questionnaire is designed to help you recognize your style and identify areas that need changing.

For each of the following questions, choose the response that best describes you. Go with your gut reaction, as it is likely the most accurate. Be honest with yourself and pick the behavior that is most like your own.

The Parent's Problem-Solving-Style Quiz

If I told my child to go to bed and he didn't listen, I would:

1. Give him a smack on his bottom.
2. Bargain with him by saying, "I'll let you stay up an extra half hour if you agree not to make a fuss when it's time for bed."
3. Repeat myself, but this time I'd go in and turn off the television and say, "Go pick a book for us to read tonight."

4. Say, "It's time to go to bed, otherwise you'll be tired tomorrow"; I'm likely to need to repeat this several times before my kids listen.

If one of my kids spilled milk, I would:

1. Yell at him for being careless and demand he clean it up.
2. Say, "No big deal," and clean up the mess myself.
3. Tell my child, "Don't worry, everyone makes mistakes," but I'd expect him to help me clean up the mess.
4. Scream, "What's the matter with you?" and most likely feel guilty about losing my cool later.

If I realized my child is lying, I would:

1. Punish him.
2. Give him a lecture about why lying is bad.
3. Reassure him that he won't get in trouble for telling the truth, and let him know that I would like him to be honest the next time.
4. Say, "I know you're lying," and give my child a time-out so he learns a lesson.

If my child misbehaved in public, I would:

1. Smack his bottom and warn him that if he doesn't behave, he'll be sent to his room when we get home.
2. Promise, "I'll buy you an ice cream if you behave."
3. Pull out the snack I brought along in preparation for a moment like this.
4. Take him to a quiet spot and give him a time-out because I believe that kids learn best when the consequences are immediate.

If my child was sassy, I would:

1. Send him to his room.
2. Give him a time-out and warn him that he'll get a bigger punishment next time.
3. Tell him, "I don't like it when you're rude; please choose different words."
4. Yell, "Don't you dare speak to me like that again."

If my preschooler woke up in the night and came into my room, I would:

1. Yell at him to go back to bed and stop acting like a baby.
2. Let him get into bed with me.
3. Take him back to bed and say, "It's bedtime."
4. Ask him to go back to bed; if he refused, I'd go lie down with him in his bed.

If my child made a fuss at the dentist, I would:

1. Warn him, "Behave or you'll get a punishment."
2. Bribe him with "If you behave, I'll buy you a treat."
3. Understand that he's scared and try to help him through it.
4. Raise my voice, use a no-kidding-around tone, and say, "Your teeth are important, so please behave."

If my little tyke kept touching the telephone when he'd been told not to, I would:

1. Hit his hand and say, "Don't touch."
2. Not need to say no, because my house is totally baby-proofed.

3. Say, "Don't touch," and distract him with another activity.
4. Buy him a play phone and hope it distracts him from playing with the real thing.

At mealtimes, I believe that:

1. A child should eat everything on his plate.
2. A child should eat a balanced meal.
3. A child should eat what he wants, but I expect him to sit with the family.
4. I should still feed my five-year-old, otherwise he doesn't eat enough.

My philosophy around toilet training is:

1. A child should be trained by the age of two and a half.
2. A child should be trained whenever he wants, as long as it's by the age of three.
3. This is the child's accomplishment, but a gentle nudge won't hurt.
4. I don't have a philosophy.

If I tell my child that she can't have a friend over to play and she asks, "Why? You never let me have friends over," I'd say:

1. "Because I said so."
2. "No good reason, I guess you can invite someone over."
3. "You can't have anyone over today, but why don't you invite a friend over for tomorrow?"
4. "Fine, invite someone over, but don't make a mess."

If I'm out and my child asks me to buy her a toy, I'm likely to:

1. Yell at her for asking.
2. Buy a toy because seeing her happy gives me pleasure.
3. I don't have a principle about this, but I don't back down once I say no.
4. Sometimes buy her a toy and other times not.

If my kids were bickering, I would:

1. Give them a warning and tell them to pipe down.
2. Sit down with them and calmly ask them to try and get along better.
3. Send both kids to their rooms for a time-out.
4. Let them work it out by themselves, but if that didn't work, I'd lose my temper.

When my kids don't listen, I:

1. Give them a spanking.
2. Repeat myself several times and usually end up yelling.
3. Wait by their side until I see that they've done what's asked.
4. Say, "I asked you to do something. Now do it!"

When my kids are fighting in the car, I:

1. Turn around and go home.
2. Ask them a million times to stop fighting.
3. Distract them by playing a game like I Spy.
4. Yell and give them a warning about what will happen if they don't stop fighting.

If I didn't like one of my kid's friends, I would:

1. Not allow them to play together.
2. Discourage the friendship indirectly.
3. Try to enjoy what it is my child likes about his friend.
4. Tell my child that I want him to stop playing with that friend but leave it up to him to do so.

If my baby cries, I will:

1. Let him cry for a few minutes; otherwise he'll get spoiled.
2. Pick him up right away so he develops trust.
3. Try to determine why he's crying.
4. Sometimes pick the baby up and other times let him cry; it depends on what I'm trying to get done around the house.

When my toddler has a temper tantrum, I:

1. Pick him up and put him in his room.
2. Give him a hug and explain why I said no.
3. Ride it out.
4. Ignore tantrums most of the time but sometimes send my child to his room.

If my five-year-old gave me a hard time about taking medicine, I would:

1. Hold him firmly until I was certain he took his medicine.
2. Tell my child why he needs medicine and offer him a bribe to cooperate.
3. Help find ways to make the medication more palatable but insist that he take it.

4. Although I know it's wrong, I'd stop giving the medicine once my child is better because I can't stand fighting.

My view of "Children should be seen but not heard" is:

1. I agree.
2. I take offense at this expression; it's disrespectful of children.
3. Sometimes I agree with this phrase and other times I don't; it depends on the situation.
4. I have no opinion.

The first answer to each question is worth one point, the second is worth two, and so on. To interpret your results, add up your score:

1–20 = authoritative
20–40 = permissive
40–60 = mindful
60–80 = accidental

You will most likely find that your answers fall within one or two categories. As you become more conscious of your parenting style, you will be able to work on it and become more like the parent you always imagined you'd be.

The *authoritative parent* values obedience and respect. Children are given clear, firm, and nonnegotiable boundaries, which is a good thing because it helps them to feel secure. But the downside is that youngsters learn to behave in order to avoid punishment, without learning to distinguish between right and wrong. The long-term consequence of this parenting style is that a child behaves well when Mom and Dad are around but may go wild behind their backs because of a lack of inner discipline. If this is your parenting style, watch out for teenage rebellions.

The *permissive parent* values love more than limits. On one hand, a child raised in this manner will feel appreciated, cherished, and respected. She knows that her opinion matters, and she feels secure about her place in the family. But on the other hand, a lack of limits may cause her to be spoiled and demanding when she grows up. Plus, not listening may be a significant problem that even bribery or guilt tactics can't solve. A child raised on permissive parenting may be argumentative, stubborn, and have difficulties with peers. Frequently, parents end up feeling disappointed with their youngster's behavior, given the compromises they've made on her behalf.

The *accidental parent* responds to problems inconsistently, depending on her mood, energy, or stress level at the time. Her impulse reaction may be to reason with the child one time and punish him for the same misbehavior the next. A child raised in this way may be confused by the inconsistencies in her parent's behavior, although kids frequently learn to "read" their parents and anticipate a response. The child will likely identify her parent as moody but loving, well intentioned but unpredictable, dedicated but temperamental. Most often, accidental parenting flip-flops between permissive and authoritative stances, so a child will experience the benefits and disadvantages encountered in both of these styles.

The *mindful parent* appreciates the need for both love and limits, and as a result, kids grow up feeling cherished and safe. The mindful parent realizes that children need boundaries, and even if he finds it hard to be firm, he does so because it's in the child's best interest to do so. He tries to understand the child's viewpoint but doesn't lower his expectations as a result. This parent recognizes that he's only human and apologizes to the child if he makes a mistake. He knows that everything he does teaches the child, and tries to make each lesson a valuable one. At the same time, he accepts his child's imperfections as he does his own.

Most likely, you address your parenting problems with one style and resort to another one when the first approach doesn't work. As you become more tuned in to your ways of responding to difficulties, you can develop a more steady and mindful response. Without a doubt, a mindful approach is the one that is most beneficial to your child's emotional and mental health.

> ❧ *According to a recent study published in* **The Archives of General Psychiatry,** *parents can minimize the likelihood that a child will have a psychiatric disorder by working on their parenting skills.*

"But My Partner Has a Different Approach"

Children learn very quickly whom to ask and whom to avoid when they want something, because few, if any, couples share a problem-solving style. In addition, many parents feel they need to overcompensate for each other's deficiencies. A mother who believes her husband is too lenient may be more severe in the punishment she doles out, and subsequently may resent needing to play the heavy. The husband, for his part, may assume a laissez-faire attitude in reaction to the authoritative stance of his wife. Marital problems are a likely side effect unless couples have a strategy to deal with their differences. The following ingredients are key:

1. *Respect.* You probably don't appreciate it when your spouse steps in or criticizes how you're handling a situation.

Whether or not you agree, stand beside your partner so your child recognizes you as a team.

2. *Accept.* As I've already mentioned, you cannot force another person—whether it's your child or partner—to change. Instead, accept that your partner is a separate person with his own style, and work on establishing a middle ground.

3. *Compliment.* Sit down and talk with each other about your differences at a time when neither of you is feeling defensive. Lay it all out on the table and keep talking until you reach a position that is mutually acceptable.

There is no question that you can change your style of child rearing by making an honest assessment of your behavior. As you learn to respond to your kids with love and limits, you will discover not only that you can solve your problems but that there are fewer problems to solve.

FROM A TO Z

The Troubles and Tribulations of Parenting and What You Can Do About Them

ANGER
Defusing It and Using It

Like most things in life, anger is neither all good nor all bad. It's a good thing when it motivates kids to do better or try harder, and it's a bad thing when it leads to destructive behavior such as temper tantrums, bullying, aggression, or pouting. As a second-time mother, Tracy, thirty-two, wasn't concerned about the temper of her three-year-old, Emmy. Everyone blamed it on her curly red hair. Nevertheless, Tracy asked her pediatrician for some advice. Her doctor felt that Emmy's anger would diminish as her language skills developed. "We gave it time and chose our battles wisely. But Emmy's temper went from bad to worse," her mom recalls. Some children, just like little Emmy, are anger-prone or hot-tempered by nature. An anger-prone child must be allowed to feel angry but taught not to vent it on others. Here's how:

Express versus suppress. Allow your child to express his anger by sulking, scribbling, listening to loud music, stomping around, or (for older kids) talking on the phone. But teach him that verbal attacks, rudeness, hitting, throwing toys, or tantrums are not acceptable. Once your child calms down, say, "Use your words and tell me what's bothering you." With a preverbal youngster, you may need to interpret feelings for him by making observations: "I think you're angry because your sister won't give you a turn with the ball."

Be cool. You can help your child settle down by staying calm when his anger is directed at you. While this may not be easy for you to do, it is nonetheless possible.

Give guidance, not orders. Instead of yelling at your child to stop throwing toys around, say: "I don't like it when you throw your toys around, because I'm worried that you'll get hurt. I'd like you to use your blocks to build a house or a bridge instead."

Promote responsibility. Teach kids to take responsibility for their behavior. Although this sounds like a rather sophisticated concept for a youngster, you can foster this attitude in day-to-day life. For instance, Veronica's son Tom loves basketball. He was sick on the day of tryouts and did not make the school team. For a couple of days, Tom could think of nothing else, and he stomped around complaining, "It's not fair. It's not fair." (I didn't think it was fair, either.) After a few days, when Tom did not snap out of it, his mother stepped in: "Tom—I agree that it's not fair. But what I don't agree with is how you're taking your anger out on everyone in this house."

FIVE WAYS *NOT* TO RESPOND TO ANGER

1. Doling out a punishment. As you can imagine, punishing a child for his anger only creates more frustration and hostility down the road.
2. Stuffing down anger by saying, "You have no right to feel angry." This leads to future uncontrolled outbursts.
3. Overreacting. A highly charged response leaves the impression that tantrums are reasonable ways to react to problems.
4. Taking sides. A win-lose outcome is the only possibility when you take sides.
5. Reasoning. Don't try to ease a child's frustration by attempting to reason with him when he's angry.

Give choices. Anger comes, in part, from feeling that we don't have choices or control over the events in our life. This feeling is more likely to happen if parents are overprotective or overly critical.

Be a good example. Learn to calm down when you're getting worked up by counting to ten, taking deep breaths, or whatever works for you. You will help a child learn to control her temper by controlling your own.

Intervene early. When an anger-prone youngster is getting worked up, use the "elevator game" to help her calm down. Ask your little one to imagine she's in an elevator that is coming down. Count the floors together: tenth floor, ninth floor, eighth floor . . . you child's anger will decrease as the elevator descends and hopefully will have resolved by the time you reach the ground floor.

Find a support group. I will often advise parents to join an anger-management group or workshop, even parents who are coping beautifully. A valuable aspect to support groups is the grassroots level of sharing between parents. Parents unanimously agree, "I learned the most from the other parents," or "I felt a tremendous weight lifted when I realized I wasn't the only one struggling with these issues."

An essential aspect of dealing with anger is helping kids to express emotions, thoughts, and concerns. Here are a few tips on how to help your kids put words to feelings:

- Ask questions that take more than yes or no to answer. If you ask a detailed question, you're more likely to have an open-ended conversation. For example, "Who did you play with during recess?" or "Can you tell me about the best part of your day?"
- Be patient if your child doesn't want to talk. Instead of nagging, say: "I can tell you don't feel like talking now. Let me know when you're ready."
- Be a good listener. Don't bombard your kids with questions and only half-listen to the answers. Look at your child, and give her encouragement to keep talking by saying things like

"It sounds like you had a tough day," or "What were you and your girlfriends fighting about?"

- Stop talking on the car phone. Some of the best talks I've had with my kids have happened while we were in the car doing errands. There's something about the car and its lack of distractions that encourages a deeper level of communication and connection.

> ⇥ *If your child is angry and this behavior is a distinct change in her personality, try and clarify whether anything serious has occurred. Speak to teachers, baby-sitters, and directly to the child. Although none of us wants to entertain thoughts of sexual or physical abuse, this must be considered in any child who is uncharacteristically angry for no apparent reason.*

Temper, Temper

Six-year-old Jack is a "spirited" child. He loves playing outside with his friends, and he gets angry, really angry, when his mom asks him to come in. Yesterday, when Jack's mom called him in for dinner, he refused and said, "I'm not hungry. I don't want any dinner." His mom said, "It doesn't matter. Get in here now." The neighbors were waiting to see what would happen next, as Jack was known for his temper. He came in. But not before using a string of four-letter words. Jack's mom let him have it the moment the door shut behind him. She was so angry and humiliated that she smacked Jack on his bottom and sent him to his room. Then she followed him upstairs and continued to yell, "How dare you embarrass me in front of my friends? Don't ever talk to me like that again. Who do you think you are, anyway?" Is her reaction understandable? Absolutely, we're only human. Is it helpful? No way. Becoming aware of how we handle our own anger is an essential part of helping children deal with theirs. Are you quick to lose your temper? Do you yell? Do you grumble and complain? Do you vent? Children learn to handle their emotions from the examples set by the adults they love. When you constructively deal with your own anger, you help not only yourself but also your child. The following acronym, A-N-G-E-R, is intended to help *you* control the manner in which you respond to your child's outbursts or other conflicts.

> ⊱ *According to a recent study done by the National Institute of Mental Health, mothers who are angry and inflexible tend to have less compassionate children.*

A-N-G-E-R

- *Acknowledge your anger.* You can't change something unless you accept its existence.
- *Notice what it is you're angry about.* "I feel frustrated when I have to call 'Bedtime' six times before my kids listen." Identifying what you're angry about will help you recognize the things in your life that need changing.

- *Gear down*. Learn how to slow down your anger by taking deep breaths, counting to ten, listening to music, writing, drawing, scribbling, talking to an understanding partner, squeezing a ball, or going to bed. Find strategies that work for you.
- *Express your anger using* I *language*. "I feel angry when you don't listen to me because I'm worried you're going to hurt yourself." *I* language makes you the owner of your feelings and doesn't leave your child feeling guilty for upsetting you.
- *Recognize your part in the problem*. "I'm sorry for getting angry. I asked you to do something without explaining what I wanted you to do."

Truth be told, it's far more valuable for a child to *use* her anger than to express it, because expressing anger doesn't really change anything. When five-year-old Kelly came home from school mad as a hornet because her supposed best friend, Lisa, wouldn't let her play foursquare, her mom said, "You can stay angry, or you can ask Lisa to come over and try to resolve things between you." Kelly learned to use her anger to take action, a lesson best learned early in life.

Take "response-ability."

Parents often find themselves "stuck" in a problem. They desperately want to work on it, but they don't know where to begin. This is where analyzing and strategizing can help parents understand their role and recognize what they need to do to improve things. It takes only a quick moment to consider your end of problems, but the benefits are significant. If you have not already done so, use the three R's to develop a strategy for responding more effectively to your child's anger.

THINK IT THROUGH

Reframe

Ask, "How do I feed in to my child's anger?"

Reflect

The following questions will help you evaluate your parenting methods. Be honest in your responses; otherwise you're undermining your opportunity to help your child.

- Do you feel you have to walk on eggshells to avoid upsetting your child?
- Do you get angry with your child when he loses his temper? If your child yells, do you yell back?
- Do you punish your child if he misbehaves? Is this improving his behavior? Are your punishments more severe when you're irritated?
- Do you understand your child's anger?
- What are the positive or negative lessons you're teaching your child about handling anger?
- When you react to your child's anger, do you tend to say or do things you later regret?
- What kind of language do you use when you reprimand your child?

Resolve

Now that you have a clearer image about your patterns of behavior, let's think about the problem areas that need changing.

Rank the issues that you need to work on from the most to the least important.

Stress level _____

Personal anger _____

Tolerance level _____

Disappointment _____

Objectivity _____

Temper control _____

Now take a moment and think about what it is you need to do to work on the areas you have identified as problematic.

Let's develop some specific goals that will help you identify the kind of changes that will be most beneficial. For example, "I want to be able to see past my child's anger and respond to him or her without losing my temper."

List four goals.

1. _____

2. _____

3. _____

4. _____

Map out exactly how you're going to attain each of your goals. Be very specific about the steps you plan to take.

_____

_____

_____

_____

_____

_____

BACK TALK
How to React Without Overreacting

"Why should I?" "You can't make me." "Duh!" "You're mean!" "You never help me." "I hate you!" Sound familiar? Back talk is one of the most frustrating problems for today's parents. Most of us associate back talk with teenagers. However, thanks to television, the movies, siblings, and a greater permissiveness in parenting style, kids are talking back earlier than ever before. Why do kids talk back? The same reason adults do: out of frustration or anger, to act cool, to assert oneself, to retaliate, to feel powerful, for attention, out of habit, to vent, to impress siblings or friends, or to push a parent's button.

Some highly credentialed parenting experts recommend that you respond to back talk with negative reinforcement (punishment or consequences). For instance, if you're en route to a child's soccer game and he gets mouthy with you, many experts would recommend that you turn the car around and go straight home. But I don't agree. I don't doubt for a second that this strategy would work, but at the same time, I honestly don't believe that you need to use guerrilla tactics to get your point across. In this chapter, you will learn about peaceful ways to respond to back talk that are equally effective and cause far less wear and tear on the psyche.

While I don't appreciate back talk, I do appreciate directness and honesty. I want my kids to be assertive. I want them to be up front about their needs. I want my daughters to speak up and voice their opinions. I want my sons to be constructive with the not-so-nice people in this world. And all of those considerations go into how I respond to back talk. I want my kids to learn to stand up for themselves without putting others down.

The following back talk strategies are based on a philosophy of parenting that's grounded in respect and common sense.

Connect versus reject. I like to respond to back talk with a question: "How do you think I feel when you call me mean?" By asking your kids to consider the words they use, you're teaching them to think twice before they speak.

Teach, don't preach. Put a spin on your child's back talk by using it to teach him constructive communication. Children learn best with love and respect. If you tell your son to get ready for bed and he answers, "You can't make me," don't get into a power struggle. Just say, "You're right, I can't make you. But next time, I'd rather you say, 'Mom, can I get ready for bed after I finish watching my cartoons?'" In this way, you model for your child how to be assertive without being argumentative and aggressive.

Be objective, not subjective. Don't take back talk personally. We all say things for effect that we don't mean, and so do our kids. Back talk easily turns into a power struggle when you focus on winning instead of guidance. However, when you see back talk for what it is—a normal developmental blip where the child is struggling with autonomy-versus-independence issues—you can face it without frustration.

Respond, don't react. You can deal with back talk in a way that will diminish it. One strategy I find particularly useful is to respond to your child instead of reacting to her. Here's an example of how to do this:

Little Johnny: "Mom, what's wrong with the computer? It's not working."

Mom: "I don't know. Wait till your dad gets home and he'll be able to help you."

Little Johnny: "Don't you know anything?"

Mom: "I know many things, but how to fix computers is not one of them."

React, don't overreact. The bigger the reaction, the greater the appeal. Your kids will stop being cheeky if they don't get a rise out of you. For example, if your toddler answers "No" whenever he's asked to do something, don't get into a power struggle with him.

> *Back talk is designed to irritate you. So the best way to respond to it is calmly.*

Talk pretty. For the next few days, pay close attention to how you speak to your kids and others. Notice your choice of words, expressions, body language, and tone of voice. Are you sarcastic, bossy, or pushy? Are you overly critical? Do you need to get the last word in? Do you curse under your breath? Do you exaggerate or talk in extremes such as "You *always* forget to put away your toys," or "You *never* make your bed!" Extreme language guarantees a fight. You, too, can choose your words wisely, and in doing so, you'll teach your kids positive ways to handle anger, frustration, and disappointment.

Foster dialogue. See through your anger and frustration and take advantage of the opportunity to connect with your child. If your child's giving you attitude, say, "Obviously, something is bothering you. Would you like to talk about it?"

Overcoming Back Talk

Your six-year-old is angry because he wants a chocolate bar and you won't buy him one. You say, "You can have a treat after dinner, but you can't have one right now." He counters with, "You're the worst dad!" How do you respond?

Don't

Warn your son.
"If you're rude, you won't get a treat later."

Lecture him about rudeness.
"When I was your age, I never would have spoken to my father like that."

Punish your child for giving you attitude.
"Go to your room until you're ready to be civil."

•　　•　　•

Do

Teach your child how to respond politely.
"Next time, just say thanks."

Control yourself.
"It's hard when you don't get what you want, isn't it?"

Let your child know how it feels to be on the receiving end of his comments.
"That hurts my feelings."

⇥ *At least some of the time, let your child get the last word in. Otherwise, back talk turns into a power struggle.*

THINK IT THROUGH

Reframe

Evaluate: "How am I influencing back talk?"

Reflect

Use the acronym S-T-O-P to help you zero in on your behavior.

See. Replay the situation that is causing you grief.

_____

_____

_____

Think. How does my thinking influence the way I respond?

_____

_____

_____

Observe. Take a step backward and notice your body language, tone of voice, and facial expressions. Imagine you're a photojournalist who has captured the moment on film. What do these photos illustrate that helps you to better understand the problem?

_____

_____

_____

Put it together. How do your mental and emotional contributions influence your knee-jerk reactions?

_____

_____

_____

Resolve

Develop a game plan of how to constructively respond to back talk. Have it all worked out in your head so the next time it happens you will know exactly what you need to say and do.

_____

_____

_____

For each scenario below, fill in a) how you would typically react, and b) how you would respond in the best-case scenario.

You buy your six-year-old daughter a new T-shirt as a surprise. She takes one look and says, "It's ugly."
a) _____
b) _____

You tell your six-year-old to get her shoes on because it's time to go to school. She blurts out, "Duh!"
a) _____
b) _____

You tell your son to get ready for bed and he snaps, "You can't tell me what to do."
a) _____
b) _____

BED-WETTING
No Shame, No Blame

Yikes! It's estimated that 10 percent of children between the ages of five and nine wet the bed, which means five to seven million kids will wet their beds tonight. *Nocturnal enuresis* is the term used by the medical community to describe persistence of bed-wetting after the age of five. According to the latest research, older kids continue to wet the bed because of an interaction of an immature voiding pattern, too little of a nighttime dryness hormone known as antidiuretic hormone (ADH), combined with a deep sleep pattern. Bed-wetting doesn't reflect underlying emotional or behavioral problems, but it may be a source of stress.

STATISTICALLY SPEAKING
- If one parent was a bed wetter, a child has a 40 percent chance of being one, too.
- Double that if both parents wet the bed.

"What Can I Do?"

- Take practical steps. If you think in terms of the bladder being unable to store a night's supply of urine, then it makes good sense to limit a child's fluid intake before bedtime. Plus, taking your child to the bathroom before you go to bed will reduce the amount of urine that needs to be stored overnight.

SEE YOUR DOCTOR IF . . .

- A child begins bed-wetting after an extended period of dryness.
- Daytime wetting is present.
- The child has pain or burning, frequency, or blood in urine.
- The child is drinking more than usual.
- The child is straining when urinating.
- There is a change in the child's emotional wellness.
- Bed-wetting is creating tension at home.
- The child's self-esteem is suffering.

- Don't be punitive. Your child is not wetting his bed on purpose. The best attitude is one of compassion, respect, and patience. This sends your child the message that bed-wetting is natural and that you are confident that he will be dry sometime in the future. Avoid subtle forms of pressure, such as offering prizes for dry nights, because this sends a message that dryness can be achieved through willpower, and it can't.
- Teach your child to respect his body. Today's kids are not raised on this mind-set. However, bedwetting is an opportunity to teach your child that his body is strong and healthy.
- Empower your child. Teach him about the body and the various factors that contribute to wetting the bed. The better informed he is, the higher his comfort level and the lower his sense of shame or embarrassment will be.
- Should you encourage your child to change his own sheets? It depends on whether there are any punitive overtones attached. If a child asks to change his own sheets, I wouldn't discourage him. But on the other hand, asking a child to change his sheets or do his laundry may be interpreted as punishment.

- Be creative in how you deal with wetting. For instance, I've known families who make the bed with two layers of sheets; if one layer is wet, then the child can simply pull off the wet sheet and have a fresh, dry set ready. Another mother I know sewed a waterproof lining into her son's sleeping bag, and sleepovers were no longer a problem.
- Do without a Pull-Up every once in a while, because a child may wet the bed out of habit.
- Beware of treatment programs that guarantee success.
- Share bed-wetting stories with your child. Say: "Your uncle Joe wet his bed until he was nine years old," or "Your cousin Sam, the one who is a great hockey player, wet his bed until his tenth birthday."
- Maintain a no-teasing rule at home.

The Doctor's Role

If your child is expressing frustration or is motivated to do something about bed-wetting, then have a chat with your physician about treatment options. The two most common approaches are the bed-alarm system and an antidiuretic hormone called desmopressin (DDAVP).

THE STATS
- By age three and a half, 66 percent of children are dry at night.
- By age four, 75 percent of children are dry.
- At eight, 90 to 95 percent of children are dry.
- By 12, 2 to 3 percent continue to wet the bed.

The bed alarm responds to the first signs of wetness by triggering an alarm. The child's brain learns to link the sensation of urinating with the need to wake up. In my experience, the alarm is more likely to wake the parents than the child (most bed wetters are deep sleepers). It will work, but not every parent is anxious to experience another round of sleep deprivation. Bed alarms are somewhere between 60 and 90 percent effective, depending on which study you read. They're most helpful with kids who are having some dry nights already, and the relapse rate is low once the alarm is discontinued.

The next option is DDAVP. The hormone works by reducing the amount of urine produced overnight, which helps the child stay dry. As with all medications, there are side effects, although they are generally minor. Abdominal pain and headache are the main reasons that my patients have stopped medication. DDAVP is both effective and safe.

Bed-wetting after Dryness

Not infrequently, a child who has been dry for an extended period of time may return to bed-wetting. Most often, this can be associated with stress or a change in the child's life, such as a new sibling, a move, a change in family circumstances, or even watching a scary movie. The best way to deal with bed-wetting in this situation is to reassure the child and work on the issue that is creating anxiety. If there is no obvious cause for the child's stress, consult your physician to rule out medical causes.

Take "response-ability."
Take an honest look at how you interact with your child around bed-wetting issues. While you may not be able to alter the fact

that he wets the bed, you can have a powerful impact on how he copes with it. Ask yourself, "How am I managing my child's bed-wetting? How can I help him feel physically and emotionally at ease with the situation?" As you begin to think in active terms, you will recognize that you can help your child accept himself as is, without embarrassment or shame.

THINK IT THROUGH

Reframe

Ask yourself, "How am I supporting my child around bed-wetting issues?"

Reflect

Here is a list of problem areas. Jot down your thoughts on each issue that pertains to you.

Embarrassment _____

_____

Frustration _____

_____

Finances _____

_____

Worry _____

_____

Teasing _____

_____

Emotions_____

_____

Self-esteem _____

_____

Inconvenience _____

_____

Blame_____

_____

Resolve

Don't get down on yourself if you feel you haven't been handling things well so far. Just identify those things you need to do differently and move on.

_____

_____

_____

You can help your child learn to accept his bed-wetting with dignity and respect.

BICKERING

Learn to Live with It, Learn to Lessen It

At the risk of sounding quick-tempered, I'm going to admit that at times bickering between my kids drives me crazy. Just this morning, my kids were fighting over whose turn it was to sit on the big couch. The fight ended, as often it does, with my youngest in tears. Many well-credentialed and highly educated experts claim that sibling rivalry is good for kids because it teaches them to negotiate, compromise, and empathize—but that's where these experts and I differ. Although I'm sure there is some truth to what they say, I have serious doubts that sibling rivalry is beneficial. Over twenty-odd years, I've come to see sibling rivalry as a significant problem with long-lasting effects. It can make family life highly stressful and unpleasant. It can hurt a child's self-esteem, and it appears to lead to aggression and manipulation. If siblings are destined to fight, and these fights are supposedly good for our kids, then parents obviously need to make peace with bickering. But I can't help wondering if we accept sibling rivalry because we feel powerless to change it. Is it easier to make peace with fighting than it is to fight against it?

I don't think so. Parents can make a conscious effort *not* to plant seeds of discontent. For instance, two young kids in my office yesterday were fighting over a truck, making it impossible for their mother and me to talk. Out of desperation, the mother turned around and yelled at Bobby, the older of the two boys, to give the truck to his younger brother. Bobby did as he was told, except that he threw the truck at his brother's head, which then needed four stitches to stop the bleeding. I'm not blaming the mother (who is blaming herself) for pitting her kids against each other. However, I think we grown-ups can pay closer attention to avoiding the ways we unknowingly provoke animosity between siblings.

> ⇥ *Be careful not to routinely blame older siblings for squabbles. Watch out for comments like "You're older. You should know better." Older kids will come to resent younger ones if you hold them responsible for joint problems.*

Another common mistake is trying to give siblings equal attention. When we try to give our kids the same amount of everything—food, toys, love, attention, or quality time—they end up feeling suspicious as opposed to content. They're constantly on the lookout for inequities, saying things like "You kissed him first!" or "Why did he get a bigger piece of cake?"

Today in my office, Stacy, a computer analyst, asked me to pretend to examine her six-year-old daughter Melanie. The mother was worried that Melanie would be jealous of her younger sister, whom I had just examined. To be sure, this is a difficult situation, and we've all been there, but a more constructive solution is to focus on treating siblings as individuals rather than equals. For instance, if Melanie complained about not having a turn, her mother would be better off saying, "I know you're disappointed that it's not your turn, but why don't you tell Dr. Cathryn about what you did in school today?" You meet her need for attention, but you do so in a way that doesn't stimulate competition.

When I'm asked to help a family handle sibling rivalry, I say to parents, "Before we work on solutions, we need to understand the problem." Then I stand back and observe the youngsters without interfering. I suggest you do the same. Take a moment, run your fingers through your hair, and ask yourself the following questions.

1. *Are my kids fighting or clowning around?* I mention this first off, because in my experience the two can sound a great deal alike. Yet only one is a problem. If your kids are clowning around and you can tolerate the noise level, then it's best to let the kids have fun and enjoy each other's company. Otherwise, you can ask the kids to pipe down or to play in another room. Another alternative is to try and enjoy the fact that your kids are enjoying each other's company.

2. *Are my kids tired, hungry, or otherwise frustrated?* Last night, Max asked Marissa if he could borrow a black crayon. Marissa, who must have at least twenty black crayons, said, "No, why should I give you anything?" My first reaction was to charge in and demand that Marissa share. But I stopped myself. If unhappiness—frustration, a bad day, not feeling well, stress, exhaustion—causes me to be short-tempered, then why should my kids be any different? The challenge is trying to figure out what's at the root of the problem. For instance, your child's unhappiness may be a result of hunger, boredom, or overtiredness, in which case feeding your youngster or putting him down for a nap will be far more effective than a time-out or a lecture on sharing. As you learn to evaluate each situation before responding to it, you'll be able to differentiate between kinds of fighting and respond accordingly.

3. *Are my kids bored?* Children like to stir up problems when they can't think of anything else to do. Granted, a youngster is likely to end up in trouble, but to a child, negative

> *Practice empathy, not sympathy. When you understand why your children are bickering, it allows you to solve the situation with a gentle but firm approach. But unlike sympathy, empathy doesn't lower or alter your expectations.*

attention is better than none. The real problem here is not so-called sibling rivalry, although it may appear that way on the surface. The real issue is boredom. Lectures on behaving won't work, nor will pleading with your kids to get along. Your children simply need to be distracted into another activity. This kind of fighting often happens when a mother is preoccupied with a newborn and older kids are left to entertain themselves. In this situation, the best strategy is to do something different. Ask your child to snuggle up beside you while you feed the baby so you can read a book together, or use a different room for tending to the baby so your children have new surroundings to explore.

> *Become aware of the early signs that your children are bored or overtired, because trouble is sure to follow. Watch for signs of restlessness—whining, yawning, or squirming—because crying, screaming, or yelling are not far off. My husband, Henry, and I have a rule to always leave outings, whether it's shopping, a party, or family gathering, while our kids are still happy and calm.*

4. *Is jealousy the issue?* Some children are more jealousy-prone than others. A few weeks ago a mother of four—two girls, two boys—came to my office in tears because her two girls were fighting with each other nonstop. I thought she was exaggerating until I saw for myself. Her youngest daughter, Molly, three, relentlessly physically and verbally attacked the older sibling, Janet. As a pediatric resident, I was taught that jealousy-related bickering happens because a child fears losing her parent's love. Viewing their behavior in this context, I realized that although Molly was fighting with her older sister, the root of the problem was not a conflict between them; Molly's fear of being displaced was the real issue.

   This type of jealousy-related fighting is minimized when you make peace with it. Jealousy is a normal emotion that we all feel to one degree or another. Youngsters, however, don't know how to put their emotions on the back burner. The best approach is a proactive one. By giving a jealousy-prone child extra attention and reassurance, you help relieve her anxiety and stress. But simultaneously let the jealous child know that unprovoked attacks on a sibling won't be tolerated. Use generic comments like "It's not okay to pull hair" rather than "Don't pull your sister's hair." Otherwise you may provoke thoughts like "You care more about my sister than you do about me."

5. *Is the problem the result of a scorecard mentality?* Do your kids keep a running tab on each other? For example, "You wouldn't let me have a piece of gum, so why should I let you play with my doll." In such situations, you can help your kids clear the slate and move forward by saying, "Let's start fresh by noticing the good things you do for each other."

6. *What's up?* Without intervening, study your kids while they're bickering (unless, of course, they're physically hurt-

ing each other). Try to figure out the underlying cause, which may be one of the issues mentioned above or something entirely different. By taking a moment to think about the real problem, you will be better able to find solutions that encourage harmony and strengthen sibling relationships.

> ⇥ *When you inspect your own behavior, be sure to notice the good—as well as the not-so-good—ways you influence a situation.*

Take "response-ability."
Keep in mind that sibling relationships are for life and that parents contribute to the shape of the relationship, for better or worse. Taking active steps to promote strong and loving sibling connections means scrutinizing your way of interacting. When you pay close attention to your actions, thoughts, and feelings, you are less apt to unwittingly foster resentments and grudges, and better able to cultivate loving and enduring connections, today and forever.

THINK IT THROUGH

Reframe

Take a self-inventory and assess, "How am I influencing conflicts between my kids?"

Reflect

The following questions will help you evaluate your way of interacting around sibling rivalry. Resist the urge to pick the politically correct answer.

Answer either true or false to each item.

I tend to blame one of my kids over the other when they fight. T or F

I refer to my youngest as "the baby." T or F

I have a favorite child. T or F

I indulge the baby of the family. T or F

If my kids are fighting, I try to determine who is responsible before assigning a punishment. T or F

If my kids are fighting, I assign punishments according to who I think is at fault. T or F

I expect my eldest to be responsible for her younger siblings. T or F

I compare my kids to each other. T or F

I get involved in sibling squabbles. T or F

My kids complain that I love the other more. T or F

Add up the number of true answers:
0–3 You're doing great.
4–7 Pay closer attention to playing siblings off against each other.
8–10 Make a U-turn in how you're managing sibling interactions.

Resolve

Organize your thoughts on how to best promote loving connections between your kids by completing the following questionnaire. Write down your answers so you can refer to them at a later date.

I need to be more

_____

I need to stop showing favoritism toward

_____

I expect too much of

_____

When my kids fight, I should

_____

The best way to help my kids feel good about each other is

_____

When my kids tattle on each other, I should

_____

My partner and I need to agree that

_____

My biggest mistake is

_____

I need to stop blaming

_____

Take active steps to help your children form loving relationships. Write a mission statement that describes your goals around sibling connections.

_____
_____
_____
_____

Try to come up with alternative ways of handling each situation:

Your kids are fighting over the television.

_____
_____

The older child won't share with younger siblings.

_____
_____

The baby of the family is crying because her siblings are teasing her.

_____
_____

BITING
Don't Add Insult to Injury

A couple of months ago, Katie asked me what she should do about her fifteen-month-old son's tendency to bite. Katie ran a home day care, and the child being bitten, little Sara, was one of her favorite client's children. Her son Brandon, generally a placid child, was completely unpredictable in Sara's company. The first thing I had to help Katie understand was that her energy was best directed toward ending the biting, not punishing Brandon.

MOST BITING PROBLEMS HAPPEN BECAUSE
- A young child does not yet have the communication skills he needs to deal with his emotions.
- Young children have poor impulse control.
- The youngster is seeking attention.
- Young children bite as a way of testing others.
- Biters like to explore the environment with their mouths.

Once Katie realized that her focus was nonproductive, she stopped lecturing Brandon about biting and no longer sent him to his room for a time-out. Instead, she followed him around faithfully for one week. Every time he looked like he was about to bite, his mom intervened and said, *"No biting. Biting hurts."* When Brandon controlled himself, he was praised. Since Katie assumed a more proactive approach, Brandon has not sunk his teeth into another playmate.

If your child bites, hits, scratches, grabs, or pulls another child's hair, I suggest you show your disapproval in a matter-of-fact manner. Make physical contact with your child and tell him, "That's not okay." Don't give a lengthy explanation, get preachy, or use strong-arm tactics. Keep it simple, and your child will get the message loud and clear.

> *I know many experts recommend that you talk with your child about how it feels to be bitten, but I couldn't disagree more. If your child's aggression leads to intimate discussions, prolonged attention (negative or positive), or heated arguments, the misbehavior will become more attractive because of the secondary gains.*

I'm a great believer in being proactive. So, if you can identify the situations when your child is more likely to become aggressive, you will do him a big favor by avoiding the situation altogether or redirecting him as needed. Close supervision may be necessary until your youngster learns more acceptable ways of coping with frustration. But you won't have to intervene or avoid situations for long, because as your child develops his language skills, this problem will naturally fade away.

> *Biting is not a sign of bad parenting.*

What if your child bites you? I suggest you respond as if your child has bitten a playmate. Firmly say, *"No biting. Biting hurts."* If you are holding him when he bites you, put him down a few feet away to reinforce your disapproval. Resist the urge to bite him back, because it may solve your present dilemma, but it will aggravate future ones by teaching kids to rely on their physical resources, rather than their mental ones, to solve problems.

Never Ever . . .

- Bite your child to teach her what it feels like.
- Punish biting with a time-out.
- Put Tabasco sauce or any other noxious substances on a child's tongue as punishment.

TREATING HUMAN BITES

Many children suffer more from the insult than from any physical pain. Comfort the injured party and then inspect the wound. Clean the wound thoroughly with soap and water, and cover the area with a sterile bandage. Gather information about the biter, such as whether he has any infectious diseases. If the skin is broken, visit your child's health-care provider; he may need immunization or treatment. Although it may be tempting, don't encourage the child to bite back.

>✄ *It goes without saying that if your youngster bites another child, you should apologize to the child and his parents and reassure them that you are working on the problem.*

Take "response-ability."

All of us cause a ripple effect when we step in and respond to a problem. Pause, even if only briefly, and think about whether you're causing a positive, negative, or neutral impact on the situation. Use the three R's to clarify the role you play, and choose more constructive ways of dealing with biting and other forms of aggression.

THINK IT THROUGH

Reframe

Ask yourself, "Is the way I'm responding to biting helping my child overcome the habit?"

Reflect

Think about how you respond to biting, and describe the snowball effect.

_____

_____

If you could hear the inner thoughts of your child, what would she say about you?

_____

_____

Resolve

Map out a plan that will help you manage biting in a manner that will resolve it.

_____

_____

_____

CONSTIPATION
Don't Give Your Kids a Bum Rap

My three-year-old daughter, Jill, complains about her tummy at least once a day," explained Brooke, thirty-three, mother of four. "Even worse, she refuses to poop. We cut milk out of her diet, pushed water and vegetables, and she's still constipated. Last week she missed her soccer tryouts because of a stomachache."

Right up there at the top of the list of problems that cause parents grief is constipation. If you've had to deal with this problem, then you know what I'm talking about; if you haven't, then consider yourself lucky!

Constipation is a problem that develops for young children around the time of toilet training. Children may become ambivalent about having a bowel movement because of inner conflicts or outside pressure by caretakers. As a result, a child holds his stools, which, if held long enough, will become larger and harder, and eventually will hurt when passed. Once pain is present, a "holding" cycle is established—refusal to have a bowel movement leads to larger stools, more pain, and a greater resistance to having bowel movements, and so on.

> ✨ *Sometimes, when a child appears to be straining to have a bowel movement, he is in fact straining in an effort not to have one.*

There are few, if any, health problems that mimic constipation. Deliberately holding back stools is the most likely cause of constipation in a child who is otherwise growing appropriately and able to pass a large stool.

SEE YOUR DOCTOR IF . . .

- Your child is constipated and under a year old.
- Bowel movements are thin, like ribbons.
- Vomiting is present.
- Your child has not been gaining weight appropriately.
- Your child has had surgery to his abdomen.
- Your child is having stool incontinence (accidents).
- Your child has rectal pain.
- There is blood in your child's stools.
- There are more than five days between your child's bowel movements.

If you're wondering what *this* chapter is doing in *this* book, let me explain before we go any further. I've included this chapter because the way you deal with constipation will have a profound impact on the problem itself. The underlying problem is emotionally based, not anatomic. When a child is holding, the problem is in the mind, not in the bowel: There is no true obstruction. Laxatives, diet, good bathroom habits, and exercise are important, but the psychological aspect is equally important, if not more so.

Diet. Diet plays a role in constipation but will not cure it by itself. Foods to avoid include: milk, cheese, bananas, rice, and apples. Milk is the biggest culprit. Try to cut back on milk intake if your child is drinking in excess of his needs. As a general rule of thumb, a youngster (two years and older) should drink no more than twelve ounces of milk per day. Meanwhile, increase water and fiber in your child's diet.

Stool softeners. Since getting a child to change his diet is next to impossible, I recommend that children over a year of age use a stool softener. There are many natural stool softeners available in pharmacies and health-food stores. Discuss with your health-care provider which stool softener she would prefer you use. I personally recommend mineral oil for laxative use for kids a year of age and older. This is not a cathartic, which means your child's tummy won't get dependent on it, even if it is used regularly. Mineral oil simply slides into your child's stool and softens it. Because mineral oil isn't absorbed into your child's system, it can be used for extended periods without concern. Give it between meals, ideally at *bedtime;* at mealtime it can interfere with the absorption of fat-soluble vitamins in the child's diet. You can use mineral oil until the problem is resolved, whether it takes days, weeks, or months.

Bathroom habits. There is a natural tendency to have a bowel movement after a meal. I would take advantage of this reflex by encouraging your child to sit on the toilet for a few minutes after meals. If she's unwilling, and has just come out of diapers, allow her to backtrack.

> ⇥ *Avoid fighting about how long your child sits on the toilet. If she hasn't had a stool within the first few minutes, sitting for a longer period is unlikely to make a difference.*

The emotional aspect. Constipation involves the memory of pain, and this negative association needs to fade before a child relaxes enough to have a pain-free bowel movement. The more stressed out and obsessed you become about whether or not your child has a bowel movement, the more stressed out your child is likely to become about having one. On the flip side, the more relaxed you are, the more relaxed your little one will be, and the easier it will be for everyone in the long run.

I want to be frank with you about some of the negative dynamics that can develop around constipation. For starters, an overdose of positive or negative attention can intensify the problem. Meaning, I wouldn't celebrate if your child has a bowel movement or scold him if he doesn't. I wouldn't sit in the bathroom with him for prolonged periods or expect him to sit for more than five or ten minutes on his own. I wouldn't put enormous pressure on him to have a bowel movement or physically hold him down on the toilet until he does. And calling your child a baby, getting angry, or using punishment, bribery, or threats will only add to the pressure your child already feels.

Your child needs reassurance that having a bowel movement won't hurt, and this comfort level can come only from firsthand experience. There are several ways you can help: 1) use a stool softener; 2) give extra water; 3) ensure he is physically active; 4) adopt good bathroom habits; and 5) don't put any pressure on him to have a bowel movement. The more calm and reassuring you are, the easier it will be for your child to relax. Let's take a moment and think about what your child will learn from your calm attitude. He will learn that he has nothing to fear; that you are there to help; that it's his choice when and where to have a bowel movement; and that you have confidence in him.

Let's take the case of Jennifer and Roger and the problems they were having with their son Blake. Ever since Blake, four, was potty trained a year earlier, he was reluctant to have a bowel movement. Sometimes he'd go a whole week without one. His parents tried bribing him: "If you have a poop, we'll buy you a Pokémon figure"; they tried punishing him: "Don't get off the toilet until you have done something"; but nothing helped. By the time his parents came to see me, they were at their wits' end.

First I had to help this couple understand how their efforts were actually aggravating things. All the attention and emphasis on Blake's bathroom habits were raising his anxiety, and even worse, they were caught up in a power struggle that they had no hope of winning. After thinking about the problem, and focusing on the way they were contributing to it, Blake's parents recognized that while they could not control *his* behavior, they could control their *own*. They took on a new attitude, one that assumed they were all on the same team, and to their relief, the problem gradually disappeared.

Take "response-ability."

Once you make the connection between your stress level and your child's resistance, you'll be able to rein in your emotions and reassure her without applying pressure.

THINK IT THROUGH

Reframe

Begin by asking yourself, "Am I alleviating or aggravating my child's constipation problems?"

Reflect

Use the acronym S-T-O-P to help you zero in on your behavior.

See. Replay a situation in your mind that is causing you grief.

_____

Think. How does your thinking influence the way you respond? _____

_____

Observe. Take a step backward and notice your body language, tone of voice, and facial expressions. _____
_____

Put it together. How do your mental and emotional contributions influence your knee-jerk reactions?_____
_____
_____

Resolve

Now that you better understand the situation, let's develop some specific goals to help alleviate stress. List four goals.

1._____
2._____
3._____
4._____

Map out exactly how you're going to attain each of your goals. Be very specific about the steps you plan to take.

RED ALERT: I know how frustrating it can be when a child refuses to have a bowel movement, especially if it's been many days since the last one and he's complaining of a tummy ache. This is one of those times when a chat with your health-care provider is advisable.

CRYING

"What Am I Doing Wrong?"

You're tired—really tired. Your two-month-old, Teddy, has been crying for at least four hours straight without relief. You wonder if a bath might calm his nerves (and yours, too). But after running the water, you go to fetch him from the crib and discover he's fast asleep. You tiptoe away as quietly as a mouse, let the water out of the tub, put the kettle on, and just as you're about to sit down, Teddy begins to whimper and squirm. Oh my God, up already? Every day (and night) I get telephone calls from frustrated, worried, and truly exhausted parents. Often a parent asks, "Dr. Cathryn—Teddy won't stop crying. What am I doing wrong?"

If a baby cries for three hours a day, three days a week, for three weeks or more, we doctors label him by definition as colicky. If you, dear reader, are the parent of such a baby, then let me reassure you that no matter how difficult things are right now, they can and will get better. While there is no cure for colic, there are steps you can take to minimize the crying. For starters, the best defense is to become equipped with solid, up-to-date information.

If you've scoured the Internet, spoken with your pediatrician, read parenting books, and asked your friends, then you already know the confusion that exists around colic. Colic is a pattern, not a disease in itself. And while there may be no real answers to account for the crying, there are plenty of theories. Knowing the current theories will help you understand why experts offer conflicting advice, and why a strategy that worked like a charm for a friend's baby may do nothing or even aggravate crying in yours.

On one end of the spectrum, we have experts who believe that colic is the result of an immature nervous system. According to this theory, a baby gets worked up by normal stimuli and subsequently has a hard time "coming down" (i.e., the baby is frazzled). Unfortunately, there are no studies to support this theory. But what fits is the fact that many babies with colic are worse off with stimulation.

Next comes the most popular theory, which proposes gastrointestinal pain as the cause of the crying bouts. This theory is supported by the fact that a colicky baby may pull up his legs, turn red in the face, and pass gas. Some doctors recommend a change in formulas or the use of over-the-counter preparations for relieving gas.

Another highly plausible theory is that crying is how a baby communicates his needs (I couldn't agree more), and when his needs are left unmet, the crying escalates. In other words, the baby's "language" is misinterpreted, and as a result he's given something other than what he wants. He's fed when he's bored, and jiggled when he's tired, and rocked when he's wet, and so on . . . Here's where tuning in to your baby's needs and learning to distinguish one cry from another is beneficial.

Last, there is a theory that says a colicky baby is difficult by virtue of his nature, or to put it bluntly, he's just downright hard to get along with (I couldn't agree less). According to a recent study, a minority of colicky babies will have difficult personalities down the road, but the vast majority will not.

The Doctor's Perspective

When a baby is brought to my office because of excessive crying, I ask myself the following questions: 1) Is the baby feeding

SEE YOUR DOCTOR IF . . .

- Your baby is crying all day and doesn't settle to feed.
- Crying represents a change in your child's temperament.
- You have a newborn who doesn't seem to be feeding properly. A baby in the first week of life may cry because she's hungry. Therefore, weight and hydration status should be watched closely at this time.
- Crying is accompanied by fever and the child is under six months of age.
- Something doesn't feel right. Follow your gut feeling.

and growing well? 2) Is he developing as expected? 3) Does he have a normal physical exam? 4) Is there anything in the parents' report that makes me suspect an underlying health problem? Just yesterday a new mother—Meg, twenty-eight—came to my office with her three-week-old son, Craig. For the past three days, little Craig had been impossible to settle. This was not like him. You know what I found when I undressed him? A hair was wound tightly around his big toe. Last month I discovered a scratch on the sensitive part of a baby's eye, and recently I diagnosed a bladder infection as the real cause of what seemed to be colic. However, none of these babies was truly colicky; they didn't meet the "rule of three" that defines colic (three hours of crying per day, three days a week, for three weeks or more).

To be honest with you, the vast majority of the time, I find nothing physically wrong when persistent crying is the only sign in an infant who is otherwise gaining and developing normally. As you can see, there is no one cause of colic, and no one-size-fits-all remedy. But chances are good that one of these strategies will help ease your baby's frustration level.

Encourage self-comforting skills. Babies are born with built-in strategies to calm themselves. But they need to be given an opportunity to develop these skills and discover ones that feel "right." If a parent rushes in and picks up the infant the moment he cries, he won't learn how to comfort himself. I'm not suggesting you leave a baby to cry it out. Rather, you must learn to differentiate between when your baby needs *you* and when he needs an opportunity to soothe himself. The next time your baby cries, pause for a moment before rushing to pick him up, and listen. Different cries mean different things. Your baby cries one way when she's tired and another way when she's hungry; she'll behave one way when she's bored and another way when she's overstimulated. By observing your baby's body language and listening to her cries, you can learn to distinguish one from the other. Usually this process happens on a purely intuitive level, but you can jump-start the process by paying close attention.

Wear the baby. One of the most successful ways to calm a colicky baby is to wear him in a front carrier. Your baby will feel your warmth, hear your heartbeat, smell your breast milk, and be lulled by your body movements. Studies have shown that babies who are carried cry significantly less than those who aren't. Unfortunately, many of today's babies spend more time in their highly portable car seats than in a parent's arms.

Reduce stimulation. As you will recall, one of the theories behind colic is that the baby is overstimulated. Yet many parents respond to crying with greater stimulation, jiggling the baby more vigorously, playing harder, singing even louder. Sometimes I feel queasy just watching, and if I feel uncomfortable, I wonder how the baby must feel. If you can't settle your baby, ask yourself, "What is she seeing, feeling, and perceiving in this situation? Would I like to be jiggled like a saltshaker?"

> ⇥ *A tip from a mother of a colicky infant: "Try cuddling your baby in a warm blanket. I coined this 'wrapsody' because it was the only way I could settle my two-month-old."*

Feeding issues. I can't very well discuss colic without mentioning feeding and its impact on a baby's demeanor. Breast milk is unlikely to be the cause of bouts of crying unless your baby is failing to grow, in which case the baby is likely crying from hunger and not colic.

> ⇥ *A pediatrician should see any baby who is irritable in the first week of life, to ensure that the baby is growing adequately.*

Remember, one theory about colic is that it reflects a tummy ache. A formula-fed infant experiencing bouts of crying warrants a trial on a different formula, especially if he is gassy or spits up frequently. Discuss this with your pediatrician before making any changes. He will most likely suggest a lactose-free or soya-based formula. Beware: With any change, there is often a honeymoon period where everything seems better. It generally takes more than a week to see if the benefits persist.

> ⇥ *Lactose intolerance is typically a transient problem that resolves spontaneously within the first few months.*

> ⇥ *In extreme situations where a baby is exceptionally irritable and difficult to settle even for feeding, I recommend a (very expensive) hypoallergenic formula.*

Overfeeding can also lead to irritability. Most babies need to feed every three to four hours but will feed more often if offered. The problem with overfeeding is that the tummy doesn't get a chance to rest, which leads to spitting up, gassiness, and a cranky disposition. Fussing may then be misinterpreted as hunger, so the baby is fed again and the cycle continues unchecked.

A Note to Mothers

Whatever you do, please, please, please, don't blame yourself. Colic isn't the result of ineffective or bad mothering. Your infant will be more relaxed by three to four months of age. If your partner is not as involved in caring for the baby as you would like (or need), then ask him to get more involved—don't think, "I shouldn't have to ask." Marriages suffer when the care of a high-needs baby is not shared. Caring for a demanding baby is stressful, and getting angry or frustrated is normal. In the meantime, surround yourself with positive influences, especially other mothers who have been there and know what you're going through.

Take "response-ability."
You are not causing your baby's crankiness, but there are ways you can minimize it. Take a moment and think about the feedback loop between you and your baby and, in doing so, learn to use it to your advantage by giving her positive vibes to

respond to. Even if this doesn't help your baby to relax, or result in less crying, you will feel less frazzled in the long run.

THINK IT THROUGH

Reframe

Ask yourself, "How am I impacting my baby's crying?" For example: "Am I jiggling the baby in a way that soothes her?" Try to perceive your baby's experience by stepping into her world.

Reflect

Although you are not the cause of your baby's colic, you may be influencing it in both positive and negative ways. The following questions will help you gauge your impact on the colic and the colic's impact on you.

• Are you feeling uncertain about your parenting skills?

_____

• Why do you think your baby won't stop crying?

_____

• Are you getting the support and help you need from your partner?

_____

• Do you accept help when it's offered? If not, why not?

_____

• How are you taking care of yourself, physically and emotionally?

_____

• Has your relationship with your partner suffered as a result of the baby's colic?

_____

- Do you try different calming approaches?

  _____

- What seems to be most effective?

  _____

- What are you learning about yourself?

  _____

Resolve

Write down what it is you need (as a bare minimum) to maintain your sanity, and share this with your partner. If you are a single parent, now is the time to accept help from others.

  _____

  _____

  _____

Become unstuck by changing how you respond to your baby's crying. For instance, if you tend to run to the rescue the instant the baby cries, slow down your response time.

Make a chart with the following headings: hungry, tired, bored, uncomfortable, and lonely. Write down your observations about the baby's cry, facial expressions, and body language in each situation. As you begin to comprehend your baby, meeting her needs will be easier.

Warning: Some babies are difficult, if not impossible, to read. But don't worry; by three to four months of age your baby's language will be easier to interpret.

Above all, realize that colic does not reflect ineffective parenting. Trust yourself, whether or not you are able to comfort your baby, because she needs and wants you.

DISCIPLINE DILEMMAS
How to Gain Control
Without Losing Control

By definition, discipline is meant to teach or instruct. Spanking, time-outs, and punishments do neither. Rather, a child learns to think in terms of getting caught: "I better not pull the cat's tail or I'll get a spanking"; "I better not grab that toy from the baby or I'll get a time-out." It does not teach or instruct the child about why it is wrong to pull the cat's tail or grab toys from his sister. The only thing it teaches a child is how to avoid trouble.

Most parents, even the most laid-back ones, have at one time or another felt the urge to hand out a quick smack to a child's bottom. According to the American Academy of Pediatrics, spanking happens at least once a week in 25 percent of middle-class two-parent families. Approximately 85 percent of the parents who spank their kids admit to feeling guilty about it later. Well-respected experts disagree on many issues, but the vast majority agree on this one: Spanking is an unacceptable form of discipline.

Many of us manage our parenting difficulties in a manner that has more to do with having a short fuse than with a philosophical standpoint. To be sure, one of the most challenging jobs for a parent is dealing with behavioral problems. But despite the difficulty, I am 100 percent committed to the position that hitting, spanking, or slapping is wrong. Wrong for the parents, wrong for the kids. Although I am about to offer alternatives to reactive parenting approaches, no true solution is possible until you commit to using mental rather than physical strategies.

Be firm, be kind. "When Jeremy, my eighteen-month-old, climbs onto the coffee table," a mom I know from my office explains, "I scoop him up and place him on the floor. Then I use my no-kidding-around voice and say, 'Don't climb on the table. It's not safe.'"

> ⇥ *A firm voice is better than yelling. Yelling leaves a child thinking, "Wow, I made my mom lose her temper. Let's see if I can make her lose it again." The child learns to control your actions through his misbehavior.*

Use words. Rely on your mental, not your physical, strengths. Any problem can be resolved without physical coercion if you put your mind to it.

Pause. With today's fast-paced lifestyles, it's easy to get emotionally wrought and lose the ability to think straight. If emotions are flying, I remind parents to put the problem on hold until they calm down and are able to think clearly. Say to your child, "We're both too angry to deal with this right now."

Give options. It doesn't matter whether you're five years old or fifty-five, no one likes to be bossed around. Children respond better to options than they do to orders.

Use the power of positive reinforcement. I realize that your child's behavior may be very difficult to deal with, and you may be tired and overwhelmed, but no matter how stressed out you are, you need to give your child praise. A hug or praise when he does well will motivate him to do better and try harder in the future.

Know how to avoid a scene. When your child asks, "Can I have a sleepover?" or "Will you buy me a new basketball?," answer in a way that will head off disappointment and whining. Say, "Yes, you can have a sleepover, but not this weekend" or "Yes, you can have a basketball. I'll buy one for your birthday."

Punish sparingly. Discipline and punishment are often thought to be synonymous, but they are not. Discipline guides and directs a child, while punishment hurts a child in order to teach her a lesson. When punishment is used liberally, children become angry and resentful, making misbehavior more likely down the road. Young children rarely need punishment to correct their behavior. If you resort to using punishment, ask yourself, "What did I fail to do to prevent this problem?"

Think like a coach. Instead of punishing your child for misbehaving, focus on teaching her to behave. For instance: If your child lies, instead of handing out a punishment for lying (which, by the way, does little to inspire honesty), teach her to be honest by saying, "In the future, I'd rather you tell me the truth." In this way, each problem becomes an opportunity to guide your child. It also forces us to think about the behavior we *do* want, and ensures that we relay this information to the child.

Understand a youngster's language. Toddlers and older children communicate with their behavior. Our job is to try and understand exactly what a youngster is saying when he misbehaves. We learned how to interpret our baby's cry in order to meet her needs, and now we need to learn a whole new language. When it was time to leave the pool, little Siobhan pulled a head-turning tantrum. With everyone watching to see what would happen, Siobhan's mom did a smart thing. She carried Siobhan into the changing room, where she could manage the situation without an audience. This gave her a moment to think about Siobhan's reaction. Why was she so upset? Her mother tried to see things from her daughter's perspective: Siobhan had been playing in the water for hours, she'd missed her nap, and it was almost dinnertime. Her mother realized that Siobhan didn't have the reserve to deal with her frustration about leaving because she was hungry and tired. The tantrum was Siobhan's way of communicating "I need to go home."

Respect your child. Lisa, a lovely mother I know through my work, was very upset and ashamed about hitting her six-year-old daughter, who refused to wear anything in her drawer. Her daughter hated what she called "girlie" clothes, and although she had all the latest styles from the Gap, she refused to wear anything pink, colorful, or sparkly. Each morning there was a scene that ended with both mom and daughter in tears. By reflecting on the situation, Lisa realized that by forbidding her daughter to dress according to her own sense of style, she was not respecting her individuality. Although Lisa didn't understand her daughter's clothing preferences, she would have to accept them. That mental leap was all it took to end the fighting. I guarantee that if you manage your problems with respect for your child as a separate person, with her own feelings, preferences, and priorities, her behavior and attitudes will improve, as will the parent-child relationship. Everybody wins.

Be realistic. One of the most common mistakes parents make is to expect immediate results. A comment I often hear is "I've tried everything, but nothing works." In today's fast-paced lifestyle, we are accustomed to instant access and high-speed connections. But with kids and misbehavior, it's persistence and perseverance that pay off.

Watch what you say. Instead of saying, "How many times do I need to tell you to make your bed?"—which is a challenge to a child—say, "Thanks for making your bed. Let me know when you're finished." This sends the message that you are expecting compliance, not defiance.

PUNISHMENT AWARENESS

- Never dole out a punishment when you're angry.
- A more severe punishment is not necessarily a better one.
- Don't add insult to injury by punishing your child and using shame or guilt to hammer the point home. You don't need to make your child feel worse to teach him a lesson.
- Punishment should not be used as revenge; it is not a way of getting back at your child for making you angry.
- Be respectful of your child's feelings: "I know you're disappointed that you can't play outside with your friends. Would it make it easier if I read you a book?"

Consistency. A key ingredient to success is to be consistent in your approach to problems. Earlier, I mentioned that change takes time. But it also takes consistency. You can't expect patterns of behavior to change if you respond to your child's misbehavior with patience one time and punishment the next. "Practice makes perfect" applies just as well to learning new behaviors as it does to learning to play a musical instrument. In my experience, a parent may become frustrated when a particular misbehavior isn't improving quickly enough for her liking, so she reverts to the old, ineffective way of dealing with the problem. However, the most powerful lesson is a consistent one.

Punishment. Unfortunately, there will be times when you need to dole out a punishment. As I mentioned earlier, punishment should be assigned infrequently and never when you're angry; realistically, it's impossible to be rational when you're emotionally charged. If you overdo it and give your child an excessive punishment, admit your mistake and ask him to help you choose a more appropriate one. This kind of approach will be less likely to spark anger and more likely to encourage the child to correct her behavior.

Time-out. Time-out is a form of punishment that is grossly overused. Although assigning a time-out makes a parent feel that he is doing something to address a child's misbehavior, the question remains: Does it work? Time-out is often used before the age of four, despite the fact that a child of this age is not yet able to verbalize his feelings or differentiate right from wrong. A young child may interpret time-out as proof that his parents don't love him; worse yet, he may not associate the misbehavior with the consequence. While an older child may understand that time-out is about temporarily losing the company of his family, it may set into motion a cycle of anger, retaliation, and rebellion. Before sending your child to his room for another time-out, ask yourself whether the tactic is working and whether it is conveying the lesson intended.

Don't make threats. Youngsters learn quickly to ignore you when you make empty threats.

Expect things to get worse before they get better. If you respond to misbehavior in a new manner, your child will likely escalate the misbehavior before he improves. A mother in my office complained that her three-year-old son's tantrums got worse once she tried ignoring them. I encouraged her to hang in there, as I was certain he would calm down in time. Although it was difficult, the mother survived this phase, and the tantrums gradually became less frequent and less severe. Many parents misinterpret the child's worsening behavior as evidence that a new approach is not working, and they give up prematurely. But if you persevere, you will appreciate changes, just like when you diet: A pound a week doesn't seem like much, but if you hang in there, the weight loss add ups and eventually makes a difference.

DISCIPLINE MAKEOVERS

The Behavior

Your child interrupts you while you're talking to the doctor. "I said sit down." "Did you hear me?" "What did I tell you to do?" "Do as you're told!"

The Problem

Power struggles teach a child that you're adversaries.

The Solution

Drop out of power struggles, and think in win-win terms. Ask yourself, "How can I solve this problem without a fight?"

. . .

The Behavior

The kids are misbehaving. "Put away your toys." "Eat everything on your plate." "Stop teasing." "Settle down!"

The Problem

You're nagging and complaining about everything.

The Solution

Choose your battles wisely. You don't need to deal with everything that irritates you at once.

. . .

The Behavior

The kids are fighting in the car. "If you don't settle down, I'm turning this car around."

The Problem

When you make empty threats, your children learn to tune you out.

The Solution

Give specific instructions and *skip the warnings.* "I'd like each of you to tell me about the best thing that happened today. Mike, you go first."

•   •   •

The Behavior

The kids are not listening. "If you can't behave, go to your room." "Eat your dinner, or I'll give you a time-out." "If you can't get along with your sister, go to your room."

The Problem

You're overusing time-out. Parents often complain to me, "My son misbehaves the instant time-out is over."

The Solution

Instead of giving the kids a time-out, take one for yourself. Effective discipline begins with controlling how you respond to your child's misbehavior.

•   •   •

The Behavior

Your child is persistent. "You're a spoiled brat." "You drive me crazy." "I'm sick to death of your behavior."

The Problem

You are hurting your child with words. Verbal and emotional abuse bruises a child's psyche.

The Solution

If you feel yourself getting overwhelmed, step away from the situation until you cool off.

•　　•　　•

The Behavior

Your six-year-old lied about her homework. "You lied. How can I trust you?"

The Problem

Your child lied to avoid a problem.

The Solution

Teach your child to be honest by saying, "In the future I'd rather you tell me the truth."

THINK IT THROUGH

Reframe

Go on a scavenger hunt for the answer to the following question: "Is the way I'm disciplining my child paying off?"

Reflect

The following questions will help you recognize whether your approach to discipline is working for or against you.

My kids don't really listen to me. T or F

I make empty threats. T or F

I am not the parent that I always thought I'd be. T or F

I yell too much. T or F

I say things I later regret. T or F

I lose my temper often. T or F

I use fear to motivate my kids to behave. T or F

I spank my kids regularly. T or F

I feel guilty about how I discipline my kids. T or F

I rarely admit my mistakes. T or F

I give in to avoid a scene. T or F

I keep losing baby-sitters. T or F

To score: Add up the number of true answers.

0–4 You're doing well.

5–8 You're winging it, which is not an effective way to manage difficulties.

9–12 Your child will likely become adversarial unless you make some serious changes in your approach.

Resolve

If you want to successfully change the dynamics between you and your child, you'll need a plan. Good intentions alone will not be enough.

List five ways in which your discipline style may be causing undesired consequences.

1. _____

2. _____

3. _____

4. _____

5. _____

What kinds of changes are needed?

_____

_____

Choose changes you are able to control, i.e., that focus on *you*.

_____

_____

Define the steps you are going to take to reach your goals.

_____

_____

_____

How will you measure progress?

_____

_____

Review goals after one week.

_____

_____

_____

Review goals after one month.

_____

_____

Task: Think about what your child will say about you in ten years' time.

_____

_____

DIVORCE
Helping Children Survive and Thrive

Oprah's show on kids and divorce hit me hard. The kids' comments were heartbreaking: "I wish my mom and dad would be nice to each other." "I hate it when my mom says bad things about my dad." "I don't want to choose between my parents." "When I'm at home, I miss my daddy." Divorce hurts. Why does this come as a surprise? Don't ask me.

I'm going to share with you a lightbulb moment I had recently. About a week ago, my father unexpectedly became ill; we weren't sure if he'd even make it through the week. Because of this, I wanted—needed—to spend every last moment I could with him. I asked a close relative, Mona, eighteen, if she would baby-sit after school each day to free me up. At first I felt let down when, in her own sweet way, she said no. Then it hit me like a bolt out of the blue—Mona, who was close to my father, was suffering, too. I wasn't aware of anything beyond my own soul-crushing pain. Similarly, many moms and dads are so caught up in their own pain around a divorce that they're unaware of a child's suffering.

Divorce alters a child. Just pick up any book written by an adult survivor and you'll see what I mean. But what if divorcing or separating adults behaved differently? What if they refused to argue? Or didn't bad-mouth each other? Would kids feel less depressed if parents didn't fight over visiting rights? And what if kids felt free to love both parents? Clearly, parents must take a greater responsibility for their own behavior and become more aware of the impact it has on their kids. Here are some of the *basic* needs of a child of divorce.

Both parents' love. Allow your child to love both of you without encouraging him to feel disloyal about either of you. This means no bad-mouthing or derogatory comments about your ex. Encourage a strong and loving relationship between your child and his father/mother. Be respectful of the other parent, regardless of how much she may have hurt you. Kids are keen eavesdroppers, so be careful not to complain on the phone, to your friends, or to family members about the other parent.

Honesty. A child may blame himself for his parents' divorce unless he understands that it had nothing whatsoever to do with anything he said, thought, did, or refused to do. Crazy and unexpected things go through a child's mind: "Did Daddy leave because I'm bad?" "Did Mommy and Daddy divorce because my sister and I fight too much?" Be honest, and tell your child about why you're getting a divorce without going into the nitty-gritty details.

Information. Is there any hope for reconciliation? If not, your child needs to know, or she may get the impression that there's something she can do to get the two of you back together again.

Stability. The fewer changes in the child's daily routine, the better. Avoid major changes such as moving to a new home or changing schools for as long as possible.

Support. Help your child defuse his anger, frustration, and hurt by showing him you understand and care about his feelings. If your child says, "I hate you. Daddy left because you're mean," say: "Daddy and Mommy got a divorce because we stopped loving each other—but we will never stop loving you."

Accessibility. Reassure your child that he will have close and frequent contact with both parents. He needs easy access to both of you, including talking on the phone without interference. Don't make your child feel guilty for going to visit the other parent. Don't compete for your child's affection with special treats or extra privileges.

Disentanglement. Don't lean on your child for emotional support. Your child does not need to know the details of your divorce disputes or the intimate details of how you're coping.

All-inclusive respect. Although you may no longer be married to the other parent, you are bound to each other through your children. For their sake, make an effort to be respectful. Don't ask your kids to relay information back and forth to avoid speaking to each other. And don't involve your kids in any money or scheduling disputes.

Be considerate of stepparents. Don't encourage your kids to dislike or disobey a stepmother or stepsiblings. These relationships are complicated at best, and your child needs your permission to accept the person whom he perceives as displacing you.

THINK IT THROUGH

Reframe

Check in by considering: "How am I helping my child cope with the divorce?" Recognize that no matter how much the divorce is hurting you, it's hurting your child at least twice as much.

Reflect

What happens when no one listens to you? Most likely, you feel angry, frustrated, and worthless. The same is true for children. Parents need to listen and respect what they hear, then make changes accordingly.

If I asked your child how she feels about the divorce, what would she say?

_____

_____

If I asked your child what the hardest part of the divorce is for her, what would she say?

_____

_____

If I asked your child whether there is anything she wishes you would stop (or start) doing, what would she say?

_____

_____

If I asked your child how she is coping with the divorce, what would she say?

_____

_____

Think of your problems as learning experiences. Write down your four biggest issues with the divorce and look for the inherent lesson.

The problem is_____

_____

What I learned is_____

_____

The problem is_____

_____

What I learned is_____

_____

The problem is_____
_____

What I learned is_____
_____

The problem is_____
_____

What I learned is_____
_____

Resolve

When children have a voice, they feel more optimistic and less frustrated.

Let's play the "what if?" game to help you think outside the box and identify the kind of changes that would be beneficial to your child.

What if your son wanted to visit his dad and it wasn't his weekend? _____
_____
_____
_____

What if your child asked you to stop saying bad things about her dad? _____
_____
_____
_____

What if your son begins to have behavioral problems at school? _____
_____
_____

What if your daughter asks for more time with you alone, i.e., she does not want to spend time with you and your new partner? _____

_____

_____

_____

Express how you plan to put your new thoughts on handling divorce-related conflicts into action. _____

_____

_____

_____

_____

_____

EMOTIONAL VITAMINS
The Ten Essential Things Kids Need

Every day parents ask me, "Do I need to give my kids vitamins?" I answer, "Yes, but not the kind that comes in a bottle." The better a child feels about himself, the more positive his outlook will be, and the less energy he'll waste on fighting and stirring up trouble. The following are the key ingredients your youngster needs every day.

1. *Respect.* We expect our kids to respect us because we're older and wiser, but kids need respect as well. When you treat your child with respect, she will feel worthy and valued.
2. *Acceptance.* The greatest gift you can give your child is to accept him as he is. With acceptance comes understanding and knowledge and a more predictable, calmer daily life.
3. *Tolerance.* The higher your tolerance level, the less energy you'll expend on fighting, and the more you'll have for enjoying your family.
4. *Optimism.* When you have a positive outlook, you appreciate life and all of its challenges. You believe in your child's ability to change and realize that change takes time.
5. *Praise.* It's sad but true that many of us criticize our kids more than we praise them. Yet children learn more about how to behave from praise than they do from criticism.
6. *Trust.* When you trust in your child's ability to master her emotions, she is more likely to become a secure child who is unafraid and better able to manage the problems she encounters in day-to-day life.
7. *Wellness attitudes.* By teaching your child that she's strong and

healthy, she'll grow up believing in her inner and outer strength.

8. *Guidance*. Children learn true self-discipline by living within the boundaries we establish for them. Inner control will keep your child safe when you're not there to guide him.

9. *Family rituals*. Establish family rituals. The more you invest in your family as a whole, the more the child learns to value her family.

10. *Unconditional love*. A child needs to know that her parents' love is not dependent on good behavior, grades, or special talents.

FEARS
What to Do to Undo Them

Fears are a normal part of childhood. Whether your child has fears of the dark, fears of failure, fears of monsters, or fears of being alone or lost, most of them are minor, and gentle reassurance is all that's needed. Before we discuss how to best handle fears, let's think about the ways we may be unintentionally promoting them.

SELF-QUIZ
- Does your child follow you around the house?
- Do you need to check for monsters at bedtime?
- Is your child a worrier?
- Is your child afraid of the dark, spiders, airplanes, or burglars?
- Do you need to lie down with your child to help her fall asleep?
- Are there parts of the house your child refuses to go to?

If you answered yes to any of these questions, then you need to read this chapter.

- *Overly protective parenting*. When we fret about everything, we teach our kids to fear the worst.
- *Teaching kids to worry*. When you continuously say things like "Hurry up or you'll be late," you promote anxiety and fear.
- *Comparing*. We teach our kids to fear "not measuring up" by saying things like "Why can't you clean up your room as nicely as your sister does?"
- *Instilling fear*. Watch out for the tendency to forecast all the terrible things that can happen (for example, "If you don't look

both ways when you cross the street, you'll get hit by a car" or "If you don't wear a coat, you'll catch double pneumonia."

- *Reinforcing fear*. When we make a big fuss about fears, we run the risk of aggravating them. If your child is afraid of monsters and you look under the bed, in every drawer, in the closet, behind the curtains, and so on, you may give your child the impression that monsters are a real source of fear.

- *Controlling with fear*. When adults use fear to make kids behave (for example, "If you don't behave, Dr. T. will stick you with a needle"), you teach kids to fear life.

The Shape of Fear

I can think of at least five different kinds of fear, and each requires a different kind of action or response. When you deal with all fears as one, you may aggravate some and do nothing to resolve others. This chapter will help you understand childhood fears and teach you the best ways to respond so that you help your child to grow up self-assured, confident, and free of worry.

The dilemma. Your five-month-old cries when Grandma wants to hold her.

The cause. Stranger anxiety. This is a normal developmental stage that will gradually resolve without effort.

What to do? Let Grandma socialize while you hold her.

The dilemma. Your toddler has started to wake up in the night, although he was previously a good sleeper.

The cause. Separation anxiety is one consideration, and nightmares are another.

What to do? Meet his needs, but as I've mentioned elsewhere, don't create a whole new set by providing comfort once it's no longer necessary.

The dilemma. Your toddler refuses to take a bath.
The cause. This is a simple age-appropriate fear. He may be thinking, "Oh my God, I'm going to drown" or worrying, "What if I go down the drain along with the water?"
What to do? Talk him through it. Say, "Okay, I know you are scared of the bath, but I'm here to protect you." Or you could allow your child to shower or take a sponge bath instead. In either case, don't worry . . . this, too, shall pass.

The dilemma. Your preschooler follows you around the house.
The cause. Children at this age have creative imaginations and end up scaring themselves.
What to do? Don't make an issue of your child's desire to be nearby, because he will wander away soon enough.

The dilemma. Your first-grader makes a fuss about going to school each morning.
The cause. Either separation anxiety or school refusal.
What to do? Be calm and reassuring, and keep good-byes short and sweet. Don't try to sneak out without being seen (see "School Refusal," page 217).

The dilemma. Your school-age child refuses to sleep with the lights off.
The cause. This is a simple childhood fear.
What to do? Allow him to sleep with the lights on. A few weeks down the road, once the fear has passed, you can tell your child it's time to turn off the lights.

The dilemma. Your five-year-old is clingy in public situations.
The cause. Shyness.
What to do? Encourage a wide range of social experiences (see "Shyness," page 236).

The dilemma. Your three-year-old wakes up crying soon after falling asleep. He's screaming, but his eyes aren't open.
The cause. Night terror.
What to do? Don't intervene (see "Nightmares and Night Terrors," page 170).

The dilemma. All of a sudden your child refuses to go with an adult well known to him.
The cause. Although unpleasant to think about, abuse must be considered. Some babies also go through a period of "stranger anxiety," starting at around four months of age.
What to do? Take time to think about the causes of your child's behavior, and speak with your pediatrician if you are concerned.

"How Can I Help My Child Overcome Normal Fears?"

When my son Max was six years old, I would have described him as one of the most confident and self-reliant kids I knew, and that's why I was so shocked when he developed a fear of the dark. One night, out of the blue, Max insisted we keep the light on in his bedroom. He started sneaking into his little sister's bedroom and getting in bed with her in the middle of the night. After a little digging, I realized that Max had watched a movie about ghosts that had freaked him out. When reasoning, reassurance, support, and the tincture of time had accomplished absolutely nothing, I decided it was time to do something a little more proactive. Max needed a nudge from me to master his fears. My goal was to show Max that he could deal with his fears. His goal was to stop being afraid. What happened next worked because Max wanted to change. He hated being afraid of the dark.

Here's a strategy that I devised to help Max. I've since used it with hundreds of other children in my practice. You can use this strategy initially to help your kids work through fears. But eventually she will be able to do this on her own. All you need to remember is the acronym I-C-A-N.

I-C-A-N

Let the acronym work as a reminder of your little one's ability to overcome fears.

- *Identify what makes you feel anxious.* Ask your child, "What are you afraid of?"
- *Clarify your fears.* "What exactly do you think may happen?"
- *Analyze and strategize.* "What's the likelihood that what you're afraid of is going to happen?"
- *Notice how you're coping.*

This strategy works well, especially with older kids who are motivated to overcome the problem. But for younger kids, or older kids who are not ready to change, the following is a quick primer on the attitudes that will most benefit your child.

FIVE WAYS NOT TO RESPOND TO FEARS

1. Don't humiliate your child with comments like "Stop acting like a baby."
2. Don't force your child to deal with his fears.
3. Don't use threats like "If you don't behave, you're going to be sorry."
4. Don't use fear to motivate your child to cooperate: "You better come now because I'm leaving."
5. Don't be insensitive with comments like "Get over it."

- Listen carefully to your child. Give him a chance to speak about his fears without trying to convince him otherwise. You can't help your child deal with his fears unless you understand them.
- Reassure your youngster that it's normal to be afraid.
- Share stories about how you've overcome fears in your own life. Here's a true story I told my kids: As a child, I was afraid of a photograph of a distant aunt that was in my bedroom. I was convinced that her eyes followed me around the room. Every night I'd take the picture down and turn it around. One night my girlfriend slept over and I forgot about the picture. The next morning, I realized that nothing had happened, and I stopped being afraid.
- Believe in your child's ability to deal with his fears. Say things like "I know you're afraid of the dark, but I also know that you can deal with these fears." Children raised with the knowledge that you believe in their ability to cope will grow up believing in themselves.
- Limit television. I can't even count the number of times parents have told me that their kid's fears began after watching

a movie or television program. Although it's sometimes difficult to predict what will upset a child, we can still make an effort to limit television to child-oriented programs.

> *Your child's emotional wellness is not determined by whether or not he has fears. It's his ability to conquer or cope with fears that counts.*

"Are My Child's Fears Normal?"

Up to 13 percent of children suffer from an anxiety disorder. The following table will help you distinguish between everyday fears and an anxiety disorder.

A Fear Generally . . .

Resolves within six months.

Anxiety Disorders . . .

Involve fears that last longer than six months and escalate over time.

• • •

A Fear Generally . . .

Does not interfere with a child's day-to-day activities.

Anxiety Disorders . . .

Disrupt a child's emotional or social activities for more than a brief period.

• • •

A Fear Generally . . .

Is age-appropriate. For instance, fear of monsters is appropriate for a youngster.

Anxiety Disorders . . .

May involve fears that are not age-appropriate. Fear of monsters at twelve is a concern.

• • •

A Fear Generally . . .

Fades with reassurance.

Anxiety Disorders . . .

Do not resolve with comfort and support.

• • •

A Fear Generally . . .

Can be related to an alarming experience.

Anxiety Disorders . . .

Are not associated with triggering events.

Take "response-ability."

Every child has her own unique strengths and weaknesses. When you understand that a child is a complex human being, with her own set of doubts and fears, you are better able to be supportive and caring and less likely to lay unrealistic and unhealthy expectations on her. There is something very liberating about accepting your child as a separate person. No longer do you need to feel responsible for her every quirk. But you do need to understand the influence you have on her difficulties.

THINK IT THROUGH

Reframe

Begin by asking, "How am I influencing my child's fears?" You may be reinforcing anxiety by focusing on fears, or encouraging fears by using them to manage your kids. Or maybe you're alleviating fears by showing your child you have confidence in him or her.

Reflect

Task: Become more aware of how you shape—positively or negatively—your child's fears by completing the following exercise. Don't give each question a lot of thought; just jot down the first thing that comes to mind, as it will be the most informative response.

I am afraid of _____

I show my fears by _____

My child is afraid of _____

When my child is afraid, I _____

I believe my child is emotionally _____

I think my child is afraid because _____

The way I respond to my child's fear is _____

The outcome has been_____

When my child is afraid, I feel _____

Look over your responses. Write a few lines about what you've learned. _____

_____

_____

Resolve

Get clear about the changes you plan to make to help your child overcome fears. Formulate each step to be something you (not your child) plan to do differently.

_____
_____
_____

How will you measure whether your plan is working?
_____

If you have already tried to help your child overcome or cope with his fears and been unsuccessful, list the reasons for not achieving your goals.

_____
_____

What safeguards will you put in place to prevent giving in or giving up? _____

_____
_____

What is the lesson you want to teach your child about fears?_____

_____
_____

What can you do differently with managing fears in your own life that will have a positive impact on your child?

_____
_____
_____

HINT: Be guided by this belief: "My child is strong and can deal with his fears."

FOUL LANGUAGE
Overcoming Unbecoming Language

Visit a playground, any playground, and you're sure to hear more than an occasional swearword. Unfortunately, I don't need to go to the school playground to hear such language. My youngest daughter, Madison, has discovered the power of four-letter words, although she doesn't understand their meaning. Where did she learn such language? I really don't know. My husband and I don't swear, and neither do my other children, at least as far as I know. While this behavior is perfectly normal in a provocative four- to six-year-old, it's embarrassing. Whether or not your child has already made you blush by swearing publicly, it's wise to have a few tricks up your sleeve in the event that it happens.

> ➤ *Small fries love bathroom talk; words like "pee-pee" and "poo-poo" send them into hysterics. A child's fascination with bodily functions is no cause for concern, as this, too, shall pass.*

The following list is meant to give you a starting point for responding to unruly language. Ask yourself, "How can I respond to foul language without making it more attractive?" When trying to decide on the best response, keep in mind that this misbehavior will disappear if it isn't rewarded with attention. Solving this problem is easier than you think.

- Let your child know that while you understand she needs to try new words, these particular words are not acceptable to you.

- Use *I* language. Say: "I feel uncomfortable with swear-words. Please choose another word."
- If your child swears, say, "I can't hear what you're trying to tell me. Please choose another word."
- Help your child express her feelings without using expletives by saying, "You sound really angry—what's going on?" or "You must be very angry. Tell me about what's upsetting you."
- You can acknowledge your child's feelings without accepting the way she's expressing them. Say: "I know you're angry, but I don't like it when you use swear-words."
- Ask your child if she knows the meaning of what she's saying. When my youngest daughter realized what she was saying, she immediately stopped using swearwords.

> *You can't expect a child to watch his language if you don't watch yours.*

"Where Did You Learn Such Language?"

You're sitting on the beach, enjoying a day in the sun with your family. Your four-year-old, Neil, asks his older sister to build a sand castle with him. She's busy reading and says, "Not now. Maybe later." And he zings back, *"You a—hole."* Everyone sitting within hearing range is waiting to see your reaction. What do you do?

Don't

Yell at your child and give him a smack on the bottom.
"Don't you ever use that language again."

Do

Think about what you're going to say before responding.
"From now on, I'd like you to use different words when you're disappointed."

·   ·   ·

Don't

Demand an apology.
"Say you're sorry or you won't get an ice cream."

Do

Respond to the emotion, not the words. (This is appropriate when it's a younger child.)
"You're disappointed. You really wanted to build a sand castle, didn't you?"

·   ·   ·

Don't

Let your child push your buttons.
"How dare you speak like that!"

Do

Wait till you've calmed down before speaking.
"I know you're angry, but I don't like that language."

> ⊰| *Monitor the television, movies, and video programs, as well as your own language, so you can ensure that your child has positive role models.*

Take "response-ability."

Reverse psychology is the answer to foul language. The less attention it receives, the quicker it will resolve. Keep this in mind the next time your child comes out with something that makes you see red. Your first reaction may be to take a firm stand against such language, and while that's appropriate, the most effective (and speedy) way to resolve it is to stay calm. Stay focused on your behavior instead of ranting and raving about your child's.

THINK IT THROUGH

Reframe

Consider: "Am I encouraging foul talk with my response to it?"

Reflect

List five ways in which your responses are resulting in undesired outcomes.

1. _____
2. _____
3. _____
4. _____
5. _____

List five ways in which you are inspiring a positive response.

1. _____
2. _____
3. _____
4. _____
5. _____

Resolve

Develop a plan on how to disarm foul language.

_____
_____
_____
_____

TIP: How you approach the problem will depend on the temperament and age of your child and the extent of the problem.

HEAD BANGING
What Helps—What Hurts

M y fifteen-month-old son, Mack, was playing with the VCR one day, when I asked him to stop," recalls Denise, twenty-eight, a nurse on a pediatric ward at a community hospital. "He threw himself down and began hammering his head against the ceramic floor—bang, bang, bang. At first, I thought he was having a seizure. Then I realized that he was deliberately pounding his head. Why would he do such a thing?"

Head banging stirs up fear in the hearts of even the most knowledgeable parents, but it is a normal outlet for the preverbal, not yet entirely rational child between the ages of six months and four years of age. It serves several purposes. First, it's a form of self-comfort. Children lull themselves to sleep by banging their head against the headboard. Secondly, a preverbal child may work through anger and frustration by knocking his head. And lastly, head banging is stimulating to a child with a sensory deficit such as a hearing problem, visual impairment, or cognitive delay.

The child who bangs his head out of frustration doesn't yet have the psychic makeup he needs to delay gratification, repress feelings, or express emotions. As these skills develop, head banging will resolve. In the meantime, I wouldn't interfere with your child's head banging, as it will only increase his aggravation. Here are some strategies to reduce a child's frustration level and teach him how to express his feelings.

Positive dialogue. Help your child learn to express himself. Let's say your child is having difficulty doing a puzzle; he's smashing the pieces into the wrong spaces, trying to force them to fit. Don't say, "It's only a puzzle." Say to your child, "You're really angry—and that's okay—but use your words."

Chill out. Teach your child to pause long enough to calm down. If your child is worked up, say, "You're really angry. So, let's do something else for a few moments, and when you calm down, you can try the puzzle again." Most kids are relieved by the interruption.

Pinpointing frustration. Have you ever been furious, yet you didn't have a clue what was upsetting you? This is a very common situation with young kids. A child may be crabby about some injustice but unable to express it. Help your child identify the problem and articulate it for her. Let's say it's time to leave for your older son's soccer game and the younger child is acting up. Say something like "You don't want to come to your brother's soccer game, do you? Maybe next week we should make arrangements for you to go to a friend's house instead."

> *Head banging is a form of self-comforting. Just like thumb sucking, it helps the child to master his emotions, which is a good thing.*

De-Stressing Strategies

There isn't much sense in teaching kids how to deal with their anger if we're simultaneously stressing them out. Here are general guidelines on how to create and maintain a low-stress home life.

- Make your home child-friendly, and you won't need to be saying no all the time.

- Have appropriate expectations. Know what is reasonable to expect, based on your kid's age, development, and temperament.
- Pay close attention: Do you nag or pester your child? This is frustrating to a youngster and will lower his tolerance level.
- Give positive feedback. Sometimes we focus on all the things our kids are doing wrong and forget to praise them for the things they do right.
- Be proactive. Distract your child if you sense trouble is brewing. Don't wait for your child to lose his temper. Step in and redirect him to an activity that will be less frustrating. This is especially important with the preverbal child.

Take "response-ability."

All of us—including our kids—need to know how to deal with stress. But how do you teach a toddler not to sweat the small stuff when hearing the word "no" sets off histrionics? Realistically, you can't entirely prevent your child from banging his head, nor should you try. But you can help your child learn to express and master his emotions. Learning how to handle emotions is part of growing up, and in the following chapter, we'll discuss other ways to help your child do this.

THINK IT THROUGH

Reframe

Consider: "Am I responding to head banging in a manner that encourages or discourages it?"

Reflect

Use the acronym S-T-O-P to help you zero in on your behavior.

See. Replay a situation in your mind that is causing you grief._____

Think. How does your thinking influence the way you respond? _____

Observe. Take a step backward and notice your body language, tone of voice, and facial expressions.

_____

_____

Put it together. How do your mental and emotional contributions influence your knee-jerk reactions?

_____

_____

_____

Resolve

Now that you are more tuned in to your end of the equation, let's work on a new approach.

When my youngster bangs his head, I plan to:

_____

_____

The most difficult part of doing this will most likely be:

_____

_____

To help me deal with this, I plan to:

_____

_____

List five ways you can help your child feel less frustrated.

1. _____

2. _____

3. _____

4. _____

5. _____

HIGH-MAINTENANCE (SPIRITED) BABIES AND KIDS
Parent-Friendly Solutions

Sam's mom came to my office when he was six months old for a second opinion because she was convinced that her doctor was missing something. Something had to be wrong with her baby. He cried constantly, couldn't be put down, slept poorly, and rarely smiled. When he cried, he'd pull up his legs, become red in the face, and pass gas. Sam's mother was worried that he had a digestive problem or food allergy. He was never still; he'd squirm in her arms and wake from a deep sleep crying as if he were in terrible pain. Nothing satisfied him. He wasn't interested in toys, hated the bath, didn't like to be held, and yet he refused to be put down. After I weighed and measured Sam, and thoroughly examined him from head to toe, I knew there was nothing physically wrong with him. He was growing beautifully, and his development and physical exam were entirely normal. However, I also knew that Sam's parents wanted me to find something minor to fix and make Sam easier to live with.

Sam was, in every sense of the word, a *difficult* child, but not on the basis of a hidden health problem. Rather, his behavior was a manifestation of his disposition. Every child has a personality type that reflects how he perceives, responds, and behaves in this world. Some babies are easygoing while others are cranky; some are sweet and affectionate while others are perpetually angry; and some are easily comforted while others demand more energy, attention, distraction, and patience. By unconditionally accepting your child for who he is right now, you will be taking a giant step toward a more peaceful family life.

Does the temperament we are born with define our personalities from the get-go? "Nature versus nurture" is an age-old argument. But as human beings, we are constantly in the process of evolving, ongoing works in progress, with temperament being but one ingredient. Society, birth order, socioeconomic factors, life events, family history, parenting styles, and personal circumstances help define and shape us at any moment in time.

While temperament may not limit us, it does describe a person's way of being in the world. But children defy labels with their immense ability to grow and change, which is why I do not believe in labeling a child as difficult, demanding, easygoing, cranky, or anything in between. Labels—especially negative ones—limit a child, not temperament. Nevertheless, to truly understand a youngster, you need to understand how she interacts and responds to the world.

"He's So Cranky": The Profile of a So-called Difficult Child

Every child—just like every person—has an innate style of being in the world. We all respond to frustration and stress differently and have different energy and sensitivity levels. In 1956 Drs. Alexander Thomas, Stella Chess, and Herbert Birch identified and described nine traits that could be evaluated and used to determine the temperament range of any given child, from very easy to very difficult. The more qualities in the difficult range, the more challenging your job will be as a parent.

Activity level. How much energy does the child have? A more active child will be more difficult.

Distractibility. A child who is easily distracted will be more difficult.

Intensity. Is the child extreme in his emotions? For example: When he's angry, he's furious; when he's happy, he's ecstatic. The more extreme his range of emotions is, the more difficult his behavior will be.

Regularity. Is the child predictable? Does he have a routine when he eats, sleeps, and plays? The less predictable, the more difficult.

Persistence. Does the child get "stuck" in either wanting something or doing something? Does he have a hard time moving from one activity to another? The more persistent, the more difficult.

Sensory threshold. Does the child react strongly to noises, lights, tastes, and textures? The more sensitive, the more difficult.

Initial withdrawal. How does the child respond to a new situation? The less open to new experiences, the more difficult.

Adaptability. How does the child deal with change? The less adaptable, the more difficult.

Moody. What is your child's disposition—angelic, cranky, happy-go-lucky, or spirited? The more negative characteristics, the more difficult the child.

In this chapter, we're going to look at how you can positively influence some of the more challenging aspects of your child's personality. As I've mentioned often in this book, you can't force a child to change, but you can inspire him to change. Here's how.

Think outside the box. When adults blame and punish a high-maintenance child for being difficult, secondary problems such as low self-esteem, anger, and antagonism may develop. The way to avoid this is to recognize your child's temperament as being outside of his control, and help him to negotiate the difficulties of his nature. Just last week, a lovely family came to see me because of concerns with Timothy, their five-year-old son: "He doesn't listen, he's a poor sport, and he gets angry for no reason." The general tone of the dad's complaints revealed a deep disappointment in his son. The more I dug, the clearer it became that Timothy had a difficult temperament. A common mistake many parents make is to misinterpret a child's behavior style as intentional. By understanding the concept of temperament, and realizing that it defines in part how a child naturally responds to events, we are able to see what the child needs and thereby reduce conflict and frustration.

Create assets, not upsets. To build on your child's strengths and minimize his weaknesses, look for solutions, not faults. Instead of thinking, "Why does my child never sit still?," ask effective questions like "How can I encourage my child to sit still?"

Be proactive. Instead of waiting for problems to happen, do something to prevent them. When you plan ahead, you can curtail problems that might otherwise be highly unpleasant.

Give direction, not punishment. The idea, of course, is that when we direct a child, we teach her and make life easier for everyone. Punishment, however, is meant to hurt. Punishing a child for his innate personality leads to low self-esteem and anger issues.

I'm not suggesting for a moment that you accept or enable misbehavior, whether your child has a difficult temperament or not. That would be catastrophic for the child, the family, the school, and the community at large. Rather, I suggest you cue in to the child's most difficult areas and set up conditions that will help him succeed. A typical scenario I'm asked to help parents deal with is a child who is getting into trouble on the playground. Obviously, you're not there at the time, and dealing with the problem after the fact is meaningless. The natural response may be to give your child a lecture and punish him. But that's not going to help, either. If recess is a difficult time for your child, you need to make changes to the conditions that are leading to the problem, instead of expecting your child to change. Buddy him up with a peer helper (an older child who helps manage schoolyard problems) who can head off problems or shorten his recess time. There are an infinite number of solutions when we approach the problem from inside out by asking, "How can I help my child succeed in this situation?"

Replace aggravation with creativity. An intense child will benefit from creative thinking and planning. Instead of reacting to your child's difficult behaviors with old, ineffective responses, put your energy into trying new options. If what you're doing isn't working, try something different.

Put a positive spin on it. Many of the qualities that are defined as difficult are truly positive traits when understood from a different perspective. Yesterday I met with a mother of seven-year-

Negative Interpretation	Positive Interpretation
Moody	Passionate
Stubborn	Tenacious
Distractible	Inquisitive
Hyper	Energetic
Intense	Keen
Inflexible	Intent

old twin girls. One of her daughters, Cecil, was a little angel. The other, Naomi, was impossible. The mother was unsure why one child was defiant and angry when both children had been raised identically. When the kids were out playing and asked to come inside for bedtime, Cecil would come in without a fuss, while Naomi stamped her feet and flatly refused. As we analyzed Naomi's behavior, I asked the mom to think about the problem from her youngster's perspective. Suddenly, Naomi's defiance was understood as disappointment. Refusing to come inside was little Naomi's way of saying, "I hate going to bed when I'm having so much fun." When you understand a problem from a child's viewpoint, you see the innocence of his misbehavior. And this is a good thing, because when you stop thinking of your child as difficult, you stop feeling angry.

Be solution-oriented. Here's where you put pen to paper and work out a strategy to solve your problems. Let's use Naomi's example as our issue. To recap: Every bedtime, there's a fight when Naomi is asked to come inside. Let's start by asking an effective question. What can Naomi's parents do differently that will minimize the difficulties around bedtime? If we think of Naomi as being defiant, we are more likely to use strong-arm tactics. However, if we look for solutions instead of finding faults, we're more likely to arrive at answers.

Here's how Naomi's mother solved her problem: She accepted the fact that Naomi has difficulty coming in at bedtime. Rather than repeating the same ineffective routine each night and continuing to hope for a different outcome, Naomi's mom changed her way of managing the problem. She tried a few different tactics until she discovered one that worked. Nowadays, Naomi is given a five-minute warning before she's asked to come inside. She carries a timer and is told that playtime is over when it goes off. She is praised for coming in, and bedtime proceeds without tempers going off. This strategy worked for Naomi and her family, but it's the solution-oriented mind-set and attitude of Naomi's mom that made the greatest difference.

_____

CREATE SOLUTIONS

The problem is _____
_____

What can *I* do differently that will inspire a different reaction from my child? _____
_____
_____
_____

Problem-solve with your kids. Children have a great deal to say when they are asked to get involved in problem solving. Not only is this a respectful approach, but it's also a highly effective one. In grade one, my daughter Marissa stopped eating lunch. I assumed she was bored with the usual sandwiches, so I tried making colorful concoctions and tasty snacks. It didn't matter. I racked my brain, trying to find something Marissa would eat, and when that didn't work, I asked her, "What's the matter? Why don't you eat your lunch?" Her answer astonished me: "We used to eat lunch in the lunchroom, but now we eat at our desks. My teacher is always complaining that my desk is messy. So, I'm worried I'll get in trouble if I make a mess." Had I not asked my daughter, I would still be preparing tantalizing (but messy) lunches.

"Take response-ability."
It's not easy to raise a child with a difficult (i.e., spirited) temperament. But in the process, you will learn a great deal about yourself, your strengths, and your weaknesses. Are you giving

your child the best you've got? What will it take for you to become more patient? Are you using what you know to be true about your child? How can you incorporate and hold on to changes that will allow you to be more the kind of parent and person you want to be? We cannot control a child's given personality, but we *can* control how we respond and interact with him.

THINK IT THROUGH

Reframe

Inquire, "Am I helping my child to become his finest self?"

Reflect

Take the "rut" test to identify your problem areas in directing your spirited child.

I often yell at or lecture my child. Y or N

I am frustrated with my child's behavior. Y or N

I understand my child. Y or N

I try varied strategies to deal with the issues that are causing me grief. Y or N

My partner and I disagree on how to manage problems. Y or N

I am at my wits' end. Y or N

I am worried about my child's future. Y or N

I can see the positive aspect to my child's problematic qualities. Y or N

I feel guilty. Y or N

I wish my child were more like his siblings. Y or N

I am learning how to ward off problems. Y or N

I have the energy needed to deal with my child's misbehavior. Y or N

I think my child misbehaves on purpose. Y or N

I am hopeful about the future. Y or N

I think my difficult child is a bad influence on his siblings. Y or N

I am too hard on my child. Y or N

I spank my child. Y or N

To score: Count the number of "yes" answers.
0–3 You have a handle on the situation.
4–6 You are responding to your child with ineffective or negative patterns.
7–10 Your perceptions and reactions are likely triggering negative side effects and further difficulties.

Resolve

Successful changes begin with a plan. Map out a strategy to fix your biggest frustrations. The basis of your plan should be about the changes *you* intend to make. Work on one sore spot at a time.

The issue I plan to work on immediately is_____

_____

My goal is _____

_____

My approach will be _____

_____

I expect _____

_____

If that doesn't work, I will _____

_____

Review progress in one week._____

_____

The next issue I plan to work on is _____

_____

My goal is _____

_____

My approach will be _____

_____

I expect _____

_____

If that doesn't work, I will _____

_____

Review progress in one week._____

_____

Write a positive term to describe the following qualities:

Negative term: hyper
Positive term: _____

Negative term: distractible
Positive term: _____

Negative term: moody
Positive term: _____

Negative term: stubborn
Positive term:_____

Negative term: inflexible
Positive term:_____

Make the choice to invest in your child's mental and emotional wellness, and you'll enjoy a more connected and loving relationship with your child.

INTERRUPTING
It's Easier to Solve Than You Think

This morning, as my husband, Henry, was talking on the phone, our youngest child, Madison, kept interrupting him with urgent questions like "Daddy, where's the small screwdriver?" "Dad, Daddy—do you have any batteries?" "Dad, Daddy—Daaaddy, why won't my microscope work?" I watched with amazement as Henry tried simultaneously to hush Madison and finish his call. Kids interrupt for many not so good reasons. A child may interrupt because he likes being the center of attention, because of bad manners or impulsiveness. Youngsters interrupt because they are wired to believe the world centers around them. However, by seven years of age, it's reasonable to expect your child to find a polite way to ask for your attention.

SELF-QUIZ
- Do your kids interrupt when you're on the phone?
- Do you find it difficult to have a conversation without one of your kids barging in?
- Do your children interrupt you and then forget what they wanted to say?
- Is it difficult to speak with one of your kids without the other one interrupting?

If you answered yes to any of these questions, then you need to read this chapter.

Teach young children not to interrupt. Every mother I know has difficulty talking on the phone without little ones interrupting.

You can deal with this situation in several ways: 1) Use a cordless phone, which enables you to carry on a conversation while keeping track of your kids. In this way you can intervene or alternatively get off the phone before your kids get antsy. 2) Think ahead. Before making a phone call, ask your kids if they would like to sit and read a book or draw a picture. 3) Give a younger child a junk box filled with interesting objects that he's allowed to explore while you're on the phone. 4) If your child interrupts while you're talking, say, "I'll help you, but not until I'm off the phone." 5) Increase the odds that your child will cooperate by showing appreciation in advance. Instead of giving a warning, "Don't pester me while I'm on the phone," say, "Thanks for keeping yourself busy while I chat with Grandma."

Be proactive. Parents who work from home or who run a home business know that it pays to plan ahead. When I get home from work, I typically need to return about ten phone calls before I can relax. I've learned that the best way to make my calls without interruption is to first give my kids my undivided attention. Once my kids begin to wander off to do their own thing, I go make my calls.

> *If you're assuming, "My child should be able to sit quietly for five minutes while I talk on the phone," you're setting yourself up for frustration. Children are egocentric by nature and will interrupt if you allow them to.*

Teach your kids to respect each other. Pause for a moment and observe your kids. Do they interrupt each other? If so, make a family policy that interrupting is not allowed. Young kids can learn to say to each other, "You're interrupting. Please wait until

I finish talking." You'll be amazed at how easy it is to solve this problem once you've tuned in to it.

Take stock. Ask yourself, "How am I enabling interrupting?" Respond to interruptions by saying: "I want to hear what you have to say. But you'll have to wait until I finish talking."

Be realistic. Don't expect your kids to be patient forever. Make certain your expectations are realistic before reprimanding your child for wanting your attention.

"Excuse Me, I Am Talking"

You have a pile of phone calls to make to potential clients, and your baby-sitter just called in sick. While you're returning the first call, your daughter is tugging on your sleeve: *"Mommy, Mommy!"* You whisper, *"Ssshhh!"* You're worried you'll lose potential clients if she doesn't pipe down.

Don't

Give your child a warning.
"Give me a few minutes of peace and quiet or I'll give you a spanking."

Do

Tell your kids before you make your calls that you need fifteen minutes of work time. Give them a new video to watch that you've stashed away for a moment like this.

•　　•　　•

Don't

Ignore your child and hope she'll pipe down.

Do

Use a portable phone, take your child by the hand, and walk her out of the room.

• • •

Don't

Put your client on hold while you yell at your daughter to stop barging in.

"Get out and don't interrupt me again!"

Do

Let your child know you're going to be finished in a minute.

"As soon as I finish this call, I'll listen to what you have to say."

Take "response-ability."

How we react to interruptions will determine whether they continue. Ask yourself, "Am I enabling interrupting? How am I currently dealing with interruptions? Is it working?" Teaching your kids to take turns, and nurturing a respect for others, especially siblings, will not only benefit your child but will make family life more peaceful.

THINK IT THROUGH

Reframe

Take a moment to check in: *"What am I doing to give my kids the impression that interrupting me is acceptable?"*

Reflect

Use the acronym S-T-O-P to help you zero in on your behavior.

See. Replay a situation in your mind that is causing you grief.

_____

Think. How does your thinking influence the way you respond?

_____

Observe. Take a step backward and notice your body language, tone of voice, and facial expressions. _____

_____

Put it together. How do your mental and emotional contributions influence your knee-jerk reactions?_____

_____

Resolve

What can you do differently that will trigger a different response from your child?_____

_____

_____

_____

Write effective one-liners that you can use the next time your child interrupts. _____

_____

_____

_____

RED ALERT: Expect interruptions to increase before they decrease.

INTRODUCING THE NEW BABY
Don't Worry . . . Be Happy

When Clara, twenty-nine, a highly successful computer consultant, was expecting her second child, she worried a great deal about her firstborn, now four years old. "What if Dana feels deserted when I go to the hospital?" And worse yet, "What if she feels jealous when I come back with a new baby?" Dana joined her mother at prenatal visits, chose her little sister's name, and was given a present for each one her little sister received. Clara was determined for her children to have a more loving connection than she'd had with her own sister. But what Clara didn't realize was that instead of helping things, she was priming Dana to feel jealous of and competitive with the new baby.

Don't assume that your child will be jealous. Most children over age three welcome a new baby into the home, and the majority of younger kids are only vaguely interested at best. Typically, sibling rivalry becomes more of an issue down the road.

> ❧ *One of the principles about how the mind works is that we move toward what we focus on. If you promise yourself you're not going to cheat on your diet, and you think about it many times throughout the day, chances are you'll go straight for the*

cookies and chips at the first opportunity. In the above example, Clara was determined to prove to Dana that the addition of a little sister was nothing to feel jealous about. She went to such great lengths to prove the point that Dana became suspicious. It was as if she thought, "If my mom is trying so hard to convince me that I have nothing to feel jealous about, then there really must be something to feel jealous about." Imagine if Clara had invested the same energy preparing Dana for how much fun it was going to be having a sister.

Stop feeling guilty. Many mothers are consumed with guilt about having a new baby. They worry whether they can love another child as much as they do the first, and at the same time they feel a sense of loss because the current family structure will soon change. Many mothers tell me, "I feel like I'm saying to my firstborn, 'You aren't good enough.'" To these moms I say, "Family is for life, and there is no greater gift than a brother or sister."

Regardless of whether you do everything "right," a small percentage of children will resent a new sibling.

Make a positive connection. My daughter Marissa loved to accompany me on my prenatal visits. She and I would each be given a cup to pee in, and the nurse would take our blood pressure and weigh us in. This was a special time for us "girls," and it helped Marissa feel connected to her little sister even before she was born.

Baby 101. Teach your child about the baby growing inside of you. Some hospitals have a prenatal program for sibling preparation in which kids get a prenatal tour of the birthing rooms and nursery. According to one mom, "When my children went on their tour, they were shown the nursery, they saw pictures of mothers breast-feeding, they played with the mother-and-baby dolls, and they came home wearing hospital I.D. bands, after which being a big sister or brother didn't look so bad."

Be practical. The fewer surprises the easier the transition. "When the new baby is born, she's going to sleep in a bassinet in Mommy's room." "Babies cry when they're hungry, tired, or bored, and sometimes for no reason." "We'll take her to Dr. Cathryn's for a checkup." "Babies have funny belly buttons." "Babies don't smile."

Walk down memory lane. Show your child pictures of what he looked like when he came home from the hospital, and tell him stories about his birth. Help your child prepare for the upcoming events by revisiting his babyhood.

Make changes early. Leave plenty of time between weaning your older child from the bottle, giving up the pacifier, or moving to a big kid's bed and the arrival of the new baby. Otherwise he may blame the baby for the changes in his life.

> *Beware of turning the older child into a "big helper." Children can get trapped in this role because they want the special attention.*

Gentle, gentle. Teach your child how to be gentle by demonstrating with a doll. The more experience she has with the concept of light touch, the fewer reminders she'll need later.

Involve older siblings. Be careful not to exclude your first child as you focus attention on the second. I've noticed many (loving) parents ask a first child to sit quietly while they discuss the new baby with me. There's nothing wrong with expecting the first child to give up the limelight or to cooperate, but delegating him to the background is insensitive and disrespectful.

Be realistic. Many parents have unrealistic expectations of the oldest child. If your youngster is not listening to you, ask yourself, "Am I expecting too much given the age and temperament of my child?"

Expect regression. Many toilet-trained toddlers have accidents after a new sibling comes home. If this happens, just say, "Oops, you had an accident." If your child wants a bottle, realize that what she's saying is "I want to be a baby so I get more attention and cuddles, too." It's important that you meet her needs by making her valued and special, but the baby bottle itself is not a necessity.

Say what? Your child has a right to her feelings. The key is to know how to respond so you help her feel understood, valued, and respected.

If Your Child Says

"I hate the baby."

She's Feeling

"I feel like nobody cares about me anymore."

Don't Say

"No, you don't. You love your little sister."

Instead, Say

Show your child that what she feels matters by saying,
"What do you hate about the baby?"

• • •

If Your Child Says

"You never spend time with me anymore. You're always
feeding the baby."

She's Feeling

"I feel left out."

Don't Say

"That's not true. I just took you to your skating class."

Instead, Say

"Why don't we read a book together while I'm feeding the
baby?"

• • •

If Your Child Says

"It's not fair. Why do I have to go to bed before the baby?"

She's Feeling

"I feel jealous."

Don't Say

"Because you're a big boy and you have school tomorrow."

> **Instead, Say**
>
> Emphasize the upside of being older. Say, "You get to do things like go to the movies and eat pizza."

Take "response-ability."

It's not how your older child reacts when you come home with a new baby that will determine whether or not sibling rivalry is an issue. It's how you respond to both kids on a day-to-day basis that matters most. Instead of putting all your energy into preparing your child for a new baby, take some time to prepare yourself for the change. How do you think the new baby will change your life? What is your greatest fear? After the baby is born, pay close attention to the silent messages you send your older child. Realize that the question to ask is not "How's my child adapting?" but rather "How am I adapting to the challenges of raising two (three, etc.) children?" Using the three R's will help you to understand your child's needs and to respond accordingly, and the entire family will be happier and emotionally healthier as a result.

THINK IT THROUGH

Reframe

Take stock: "How am I handling the complexities of having another child?"

Reflect

Write a letter to each of your children about her unique position in the family.

Dear _____

_____

_____

_____

_____

_____

_____

Resolve

Write a mission statement about your parenting goals
relating to sibling relationships. _____

_____

_____

_____

_____

_____

_____

_____

_____

JEALOUSY
Stop Seeing Red

When five-year-old Rachel realized that her baby sister stayed at home while she went off to school, she complained, "Why does Kayla get to stay home? It's not fair. You spend all your time with Kayla." What should you say or do? The three R's can help you work through the problem.

THINK IT THROUGH

Reframe

"How am I managing my child's tendency toward jealousy?"

Reflect

Use the acronym S-T-O-P to help you zero in on your behavior.

See. Replay the situation in your mind that is causing you grief. Pay close attention to the feedback loop between you and your daughter. _____

_____

Think. How does your thinking influence the way you respond? You can't understand what your daughter's complaining about given that she adores school. _____

_____

Observe. Take a step backward and notice your body language, tone of voice, and facial expressions. No problems in this arena—you are warm and loving._____

_____

Put it together. How do your mental and emotional contributions influence your knee-jerk reactions? You feel guilty. Maybe you haven't been giving your daughter enough attention. Or enough for her, anyway. _____

_____

Resolve

Use this as an opportunity to connect with your child by saying, "Sometimes it's hard being the older sister. But there are good parts, too—like you get to stay up later at night."

Let your child know it's okay to feel jealous. Identify with her by saying, "Sometimes I feel jealous, too."

You plan to pay closer attention to whether you're (unknowingly) delegating your older child to the background and thereby giving her reason to feel jealous.

HINT: You have a powerful influence on the quality of the relationship between siblings. Use this power wisely.

KVETCHING (COMPLAINING)

How to Raise Appreciative Kids

Complain, complain, complain . . . no matter how hard you try, some kids just never stop complaining. Many of today's kids are growing up believing, "It's my right to get whatever I want, whenever I want it." In fact, today's consumer society actually teaches our kids to feel this way by valuing material goods over people. Six-year-old Helen's parents were disappointed when she complained about her birthday cake—"I wish I had a chocolate cake"—and then she found fault with the entertainment—"Why didn't you get a magician?"—and the final straw was when she grumbled about her presents: "I didn't get anything I wanted." How can these parents help little Helen to be more grateful, respectful, and appreciative?

THINK IT THROUGH

Reframe

Ask yourself, "How am I influencing my child's tendency to complain?"

Reflect

Good manners teach kids to value the things others do for them. Are you setting a good example?

What is the payoff of complaining for your child?

_____

_____

_____

Why do you respond to your child's complaints as you do?

_____

_____

Resolve

Think up responses to your child's gripes that will guide or direct her. For instance, say, "Helen, I'd rather you just say, 'Thanks for the great party.'" _____

_____

_____

RED ALERT: Don't forget to acknowledge the good things your child does on a day-to-day basis, and express appreciation for the mere fact that she's your child.

LIES, FIBS, DECEPTIONS
The Key to Raising Honest Kids

I brushed my teeth," five-year-old Katie promised. Yet when her dad went in the bathroom to check, he found her toothbrush dry.

"I did all my homework," said six-year-old Mark. Why, then, did he come home with a note from his teacher about unfinished schoolwork?

"I didn't spill the juice," insist all three of my kids. Yet I know full well that one of them did.

There's a fuzzy line between reality and wishful thinking when it comes to toddlers and preschoolers. Sometimes they want something so badly that they actually believe in it. For instance, when Lilly asked her four-year-old son Tom why he came home from a play date with a toy that didn't belong to him, Tom answered, "Leo said I could borrow it." Imagine Lilly's embarrassment when she returned the toy the next day and discovered that Leo had been looking for it all morning. Spinning yarns is another form of lying that is common at this age. Just yesterday I heard three-and-a-half-year-old David tell another child in my waiting room that I'd just given him a needle. He claimed, "I didn't cry." I had to laugh, because not only did I not give this child a needle, I hadn't forgotten the last time I did. My nurse had to chase him around the office twice before she was able to give him his immunization.

Older kids lie to avoid punishment, please parents, and solve problems. For example, six-year-old Jeremy told his parents, "All the boys in my class were sent to the principal's office. But I didn't have to go. I promise." The next day, however, the principal called for a meeting to discuss Jeremy's behavior.

Is Honesty the Best Policy?

Adults tell many white lies in the course of a day that give the impression that lying is an acceptable way to overcome problems. If you're anything like other parents I know, as you begin to pay closer attention, you'll discover you tell white lies more often than you ever imagined.

WHITE LIES THROUGH CHILDREN'S EYES

If you do this . . .

Your daughter doesn't want to talk to someone on the phone, so you lie for her and say she's not home.

She learns . . .

It's okay to lie to friends.

. . .

If you do this . . .

Your daughter doesn't finish her homework, so you write a note to the teacher saying she was sick.

She learns . . .

Lying solves problems.

. . .

If you do this . . .

Your kids are bugging you for a soda pop, and instead of saying no, you hide what's left and pretend it's all gone.

> **She learns . . .**
>
> They learn not to trust you.

> ⊱ *Are white lies ever acceptable? I think the only time a white lie is not a bad idea is when a child receives a gift and pretends to like it, even if he doesn't.*

What to Do?

Don't label your child a liar, use harsh words, or punish her for minor offenses. The heavier you come down on her, the more likely she is to lie in the future in order to avoid punishment. Instead, praise your child for fessing up to her mistakes. I will never forget the time when I was a young child and I broke my mother's favorite strand of pearls. I knew perfectly well that I was not allowed to play with her jewelry. But one night when she and my father went out for dinner, I couldn't resist. Almost immediately, the string broke and the pearls scattered everywhere. Although I was petrified to tell my mother, there was no way out. I will never forget her reaction. She thanked me for being honest. The next day my mother had the pearls restrung and gave me the necklace soon after. To this day, each time I wear the necklace I think of her wisdom.

Appreciate honesty. We have a policy in our home: If our kids are honest about their mistakes, we don't reprimand them. The best way to encourage honesty is to make youngsters feel safe telling the truth. Don't trigger lies by asking questions if you already know the answer. If you know your three-year-old didn't brush his teeth, don't ask him. Instead, say, "I can see you haven't brushed your teeth. Please do it now."

Don't call your child a liar. If you do, he will have no motivation to tell the truth because lying is what is expected of him.

> ❧ *If you punish, get angry, or lecture your child when he tells the truth, you're prompting him to lie in the future. Teach your kids that honesty is the best policy by not punishing your youngster when he tells the truth.*

Total acceptance. Give your child unconditional love and acceptance. When children feel accepted, they are less likely to feel the need to embellish.

Admit your mistakes. Practice what you preach. If you overreact to something your child says or does, swallow your pride and apologize to her for overreacting. This teaches her that we all make mistakes and models how to acknowledge faults without blaming others or making excuses.

IF YOUR CHILD LIES

Don't

Say to him, "You're a liar."

Do

Acknowledge the truth and move on.

· · ·

Don't

Send your child to his room for a time-out.

Do

Look for solutions, not faults. "I can see you spilled the milk. Please clean it up."

. . .

Don't

Tell your child, "If you keep lying, you'll end up in jail."

Do

Coach your child: "One of you made a mess. Whoever did it, please tidy up."

. . .

Don't

Say, "I promise you won't get in trouble if you tell the truth."

Do

Think ahead. Say, "Next time, if you get sent to the office, I would rather you tell me the truth."

Take "response-ability."

How you respond to lying will shape your child's willingness to tell the truth in the future. Instead of playing the heavy, you can accept that your child made a mistake and help him move forward. When you do, you'll be rewarded with an honest child who is not afraid to turn to you for help.

THINK IT THROUGH

Reframe

Pause for a moment and think about this: "How am I shaping my child's tendency to lie?"

Reflect

Analyze whether your child is getting the message that the truth will land him in trouble. Picture exactly what it is you do that may be giving him the wrong impression.

When my child tells a lie, I say _____
_____
_____

This teaches my child that _____
_____
_____

What I'm doing that's helping is _____
_____
_____

What I'm doing that's hurting is _____
_____
_____

I'm worried that _____
_____
_____

I feel_____
_____
_____

I think _____

_____

Resolve

Encourage honesty by teaching your child it's safe to tell the truth. Put your insight into action by devising how to constructively respond to future fibs and tall tales.

Your five-year-old promises he brushed his teeth, but his toothbrush is dry.

Your knee-jerk reaction is _____

_____

But you rise above this response and _____

_____

_____

Your six-year-old says he didn't take the toy from the baby. But it's gone, and he's the only one home besides you.

Your knee-jerk reaction is to say _____

_____

But you rise above this response and say _____

_____

_____

LISTENING
What Works—What Doesn't

W hen I ask Jacob to stop pulling the cat's tail, he ignores me," complained twenty-two-year-old Nancy. "When I warn him, 'If you do it again, you'll get a time-out,' he pretends not to hear me. When I say, 'How would you like it if I pulled your hair?,' he doesn't answer me. How do I get through to him?"

I'd say that not listening is right up there at the top of the list of parenting complaints. Adults expend an enormous amount of energy trying to get their kids to listen, but all too often they go about it in the wrong way. Let's look at the problem, beginning with what *not* to do.

Don't yell. The more you yell, the less it means, the worse you feel about losing control, the better kids feel about running the show. I'm not suggesting kids are intentionally manipulative, but ineffective habits breed ineffective attitudes. Typically, adults yell when they run out of other options; while it may solve the current dilemma, it does nothing to encourage better listening down the road.

> *I encourage parents to take a time-out themselves when they're all worked up. The idea behind taking a time-out is to give your emotions a moment to unwind, and it allows you to gain some perspective and control over your actions and words. Sound familiar? I urge parents to become aware of*

> *their early warning signs and learn to take a time-out before emotions are flying. In that way, you can avoid behaving in ways you later regret.*

Don't bargain with or bribe your kids. If you ask me what I think is one of the worst parenting mistakes, I'd say bribing kids to cooperate. When we bribe kids to cooperate, they learn to think, "Okay, should I cooperate or hold out for more?" Soon adults find themselves wheeling and dealing for an ounce of cooperation.

Don't nag. Kids quickly become parent-deaf when they feel pestered.

Don't make threats, especially empty ones. Kids learn that most threats never happen and that, for the most part, they can ignore them.

Don't rely on punitive methods. Spanking, time-out, punishment, and yelling do not inspire good listening. Instead, they promote anger, antagonism, power struggles, and greater problems down the road.

> ✑ *Think of your child as programmed to push the limits. You'll be less frustrated, and better able to respond with love and laughter, if you expect him/her to question and rebel against everything he's asked to do.*

"Don't Make Me Ask You Again"

The bottom line is this: *Kids don't listen because we allow them not to.* If you ask your child to do something and then walk away, you're inviting her to ignore you. In effect, you're saying, "I want you to listen, although I know full well you won't." Instead of issuing warnings—which go in one ear and out the other—ask your child to do something and then stay put until it's done. Kids need to be taught to listen, not get yelled at when they don't. To avoid a power struggle, help your child do whatever it is you're asking and then gradually ease your way out of this role.

THE A, B, C, AND D'S OF LISTENING

I promise you that your kids will no longer suffer from selective hearing once you've made it crystal-clear that tuning you out is not an option.

- *Ask* in a no-kidding-around tone of voice.
- *Be* clear and specific.
- *Communicate* your request in six words or less.
- *Don't* make not listening an option.

Be proactive. For instance, give yourself extra time in the morning if getting the kids off to school is a problem. The calmer you feel, the easier it will be to gently guide your kids toward becoming better listeners.

Set limits. Toddlers feel out of control and unprotected when parents don't set enough limits. Imagine the chaos and confusion that would exist without stop signs. Every corner would pose a hazard. Should you stop? Go? Slow down? Limits make the world safe and free us to act without consequences. The same goes for children's limits.

Create rituals. Children respond well to routines and will respect the rules of the routine without a rebellion. Children benefit from predictability and repetition. If you always do the same things in the same order, kids think, "Okay, I've brushed my teeth, which means that now it's time to wash my face, and then it's time for me to go to bed. Good night."

Try making a poster that walks your child through each step of the routine. If your child is resistant, refer to the poster. When the poster becomes the authority, the child is less likely to rebel.

> ⇥ *Many children truly don't know that "No means no." We inadvertently promote pestering by giving in to it. This sends the message that it pays to be persistent. If this sounds familiar, ask yourself, "Why do I find it hard to be firm or say no to my kids?"*

Realistic expectations. If what you are asking your child to do is unreasonable, not listening is a likely outcome. Parents trick themselves into thinking they're being realistic when they're not. Before requesting something of your child a second time, ask yourself, "Am I being realistic?" For instance: You shouldn't expect a four-year-old to sit quietly, without anything to do, while you speak to the doctor; it will most likely lead to fighting and frustration.

Be straightforward. Watch out for ambiguous messages. Here are a few examples of how parents try and sneak something in the back door that they're afraid to bring in through the front door:

Mixed Message

"You can play with that toy later, but not now."

Clear Message

"It's time to put the toy away."

Mixed Message

"We'll go swimming tomorrow if you leave now without making a fuss."

Clear Message

"It's time to go."

• • •

Mixed Message

"If you pull the cat's tail one more time, I'm going to pull your hair and show you how it feels."

Clear Message

"Please stop pulling the cat's tail."

"Read My Lips"

To teach good listening habits, you must talk to your children in a way that doesn't turn them off or encourage them to tune you out. The following tactics will help you communicate calmly and effectively, which is a key ingredient in teaching children to listen.

Many parents give lengthy explanations and justifications when they ask their kids to do something, which becomes a significant source of stress. Kids learn to stall by asking questions. "Why do I have to go to bed now? Why doesn't Janice have to go to bed now? What is sleep?" Just imagine the energy it takes to answer these questions. And the worst part of it is that when you finally put your foot down and refuse to answer any more questions, most kids resist all the same. My advice to you is this: As with the title of any best-seller, keep your instructions to no more than six words.

Your child is more likely to listen if you give him specific instructions. Instead of saying, "Clean up your room," tell him exactly what it is you'd like him to do: "Pick up the clothes that are on the floor and then put your crayons in the box." Don't ask your child to do something with a question, such as "Would you mind putting your shoes on now?" This is an invitation for the child to say, "Yes, I do mind. I'm busy watching my favorite cartoons. Come back later and I'll let you know if I'm free." Rephrase your request in statement form: for instance, "Please put your shoes on now."

Preverbal children need to be shown what you want them to do. If you want a toddler to learn to put away his toys, get down on the floor and put them away with him. Pass the toys to your child and ask him to figure out where to put them; race to see who can put away the most toys; or simply put the toys away as a team. If your child refuses to help, then hold him on your hip as you pick up a few toys; thank him for helping when you're finished. Your child will want to help out sooner or later.

Ensure that you have your child's full attention before you speak, or ask your child if he's listening before asking him to do something. Finally, remember to be respectful. If you ask your child to do something and he says, "Can I do it when I finish building my LEGO?," look at the situation from his point of view before you zap back with "Do as you're told." If you can respect his requests, then do so, because this teaches him two important lessons: 1) that what the child wants matters, and 2) compromise is a valuable way to resolve problems.

Listening Up

You call out "Bedtime," but your kids pretend not to hear. One of your kids is playing on the computer, another is watching a video, and the youngest is complaining, "It's too early to go to bed." You raise your voice and issue a warning: *"Get to bed now or else!"* Your kids don't budge. What do you do?

Don't

Give a final warning.
"If you don't get to bed this instant, there'll be no television for a week."

Do

Stop issuing warnings; wait until each child has done what he's been asked before walking away.
"Okay, pumpkin, let's go. Turn off the television and choose a bedtime story."

· · ·

Don't

Get very angry and tell your husband to put the kids to bed.
"You put them to bed. They won't listen to me."

Do

Give a warning.
"It's bedtime in ten minutes. When the clock says seven-thirty, come and get me so I can tuck you in."

· · ·

Don't

Let your kids fall asleep on the couch because they refuse to go to bed.

"Fine. Go to sleep wherever you want."

Do

Give them motivation to listen.

"Let's see if you can get in your pajamas before I count to ten."

❧ *Parent and child participate in "not listening" together. On the one end of the equation is the child who has selective hearing, and on the other is the parent who reinforces the behavior by allowing it to happen. By understanding your part, you will know what you need to do differently in order to solve the problem.*

Take "response-ability."

All parents want their kids to listen. But what many of us fail to realize is that we may be inadvertently teaching them to ignore us. Before you can work on it, you need to understand precisely what kind of problem you have. Do you give too many orders? Do you make empty threats? Do you give your kids room to ignore you? Are you busy waiting for your kids to change instead of changing yourself? Use the A, B, C, and D's of listening and the three R's to help acknowledge the changes you need to make and come up with a plan to put your newfound insights into action.

THINK IT THROUGH

Reframe

Begin by asking yourself, "In what ways do I allow or invite my kids not to listen to me?"

Reflect

What are you doing (or not doing) to give your child the impression that he can ignore you?

Do you give orders and walk away? Y or N

Do you lecture your child about not listening? Y or N

Have you wondered if your child has a hearing problem? Y or N

Do your kids ignore you unless you yell? Y or N

Do you punish your child for not listening? Y or N

Do you make threats about what will happen if your child doesn't listen to you? Y or N

Do you bribe your kids to listen? Y or N

Do you need to repeat yourself more than three times? Y or N

Count the number of "yes" answers.
0–3 Your kids are listening most of the time.
3–5 You have the situation under control, but fine-tuning is needed.
5 or more Your kids are not listening. Rethink your approach to the problem.

Resolve

Your child is not going to become a better listener just because you want him to. What can you do differently that will inspire a different reaction? _____

_____

_____

_____

You tell your four-year-old to stop playing with the remote control. He totally ignores you.

Your knee-jerk reaction is _____

_____

But you pause, think, and then say _____

_____

You ask your kids to turn off the television and nothing happens. You say it again, and your kids pretend not to hear you.

Your knee-jerk reaction is _____

_____

But you pause, think, and then say _____

_____

RED ALERT: Describe the changes in terms of what *you* need to do differently.

MEDICINE
What to Do When Your Child Refuses

Have you ever tried to give medicine to a child who refuses to open her mouth? Or tried to use an inhaler with a child who won't sit still? What about eyedrops, which can be a challenge for even the most experienced parents? And how do you put cream on a child who squirms? Jill's middle child, Charlie, was diagnosed with a throat infection on his sixth birthday. She left the doctor's office with a prescription and was instructed to give Charlie one spoonful of antibiotic three times a day. As long as Charlie took the medication, his party could proceed as planned. But there was only one problem: Charlie refused to take his medication. "It tastes horrible," he complained. And there was no convincing him otherwise.

WHY KIDS MAY REFUSE TO TAKE MEDICATION
- The high syrup content is unpleasant for many children.
- A preverbal child does not understand the concept of medicine.
- A three- to four-year-old is trying out his newfound independence.
- Older kids may rebel on principle.

"A Spoonful of Sugar Helps the Medicine Go Down"

The following tips have been pretested on thousands of formerly frustrated parents whose children are now willingly taking medication when needed.

- One creative mother, Janice, a cake designer, shared this strategy with me. Her three-year-old daughter, Sky, loved Barney. Sky slept hugging a Barney pillow; she walked around with a Barney blanket; and she carried her toys in a Barney backpack. About a month ago, Sky came down with a fever and needed an antibiotic. After discussing the idea with her pharmacist, Sky's mom added purple food coloring to the antibiotic. And guess what happened? Sky, for the first time ever, gulped "Barney medicine" without putting up a fight.

- A Popsicle before and after medication helps even the most noxious medicine go down. Some parents claim that a gulp of pancake syrup is a more effective way to mask a bad taste, which makes good sense because syrup will coat the tongue and the taste buds. You can also try a spoonful of chocolate syrup as a chaser.

- Rinse a spoon in water, and liquid medication will slide off quickly and smoothly.

- Give medication by hiding it in a spoonful of food, which dilutes the taste. If a smaller amount of medicine is hidden in several spoonfuls of food, the taste will be even less recognizable. Check with your pharmacist before doing this, as some medications need to be taken on an empty stomach.

- Bypass your baby's taste buds by squirting the medicine into the fat pads at the side of his mouth.

WHEN YOUR CHILD REFUSES MEDICINE

What It May Mean

I'm not hungry.

What It Doesn't Mean

I'm being difficult to get back at you.

·   ·   ·

What It May Mean

I hate the taste.

What It Doesn't Mean

I'm the boss.

· · ·

What It May Mean

I'm confused.

What It Doesn't Mean

I'm trying to irritate you.

· · ·

What It May Mean

My tummy feels yucky.

What It Doesn't Mean

I hate medicine.

· · ·

What It May Mean

I'm tired.

What It Doesn't Mean

I want you to worry.

· · ·

What It May Mean

I don't understand.

What It Doesn't Mean

I want to make you angry.

- Buy a medication dispenser. There are some ingenious pacifier-style dispensers that "squirt" medications in small amounts. These are available on the Internet and in some pharmacies and baby-supply stores. A syringe-type medication dispenser is available in most pharmacies (see "Resources," page 333).
- My kids are more willing to take medication if I allow them to measure it themselves. I also ask my kids to remind me when it's time for their next dose.
- Jackie, the mother of five-year-old twin boys, gives them medicine while they're playing in the bath. "The kids are distracted by their bath toys, they are contained by the bath, and soap and water is within easy reach in case of a spill."
- For kids who are super-resistant, find a pharmacist who is able to alter the taste of the medication or prepare it in an alternative form. I've found a pharmacist who is willing and able to do this for my patients. He can prepare an antibiotic so it can be given as a lollipop or looks and tastes like a gummy bear. Ask your doctor if he knows of such a pharmacist in your area.
- If your child refuses to stand still long enough to apply a cream, try using a paintbrush or sponge. Most kids love body painting.
- Inhalers a problem? Try facing a mirror. Or sit your child in front of the television with his favorite video playing. Yesterday I watched as one mother in my office played a trumpet game; she pretended the puffer and mask was an instrument the child was playing. When all else fails, wrap your child in a blanket and give him a "hug and a kiss"— the blanket hugs the child and the inhaler is a kiss. Let your child decorate his inhaler to make it more child-friendly.

- How about eyedrops? Ask the child to lie down and close his eyes, then drop the medication in the inner corner of the eye nearest to the nose. Then have the child open his eyes, and the medication will roll in. Add in a game of peekaboo and you're home free.
- Here's an ingenious (and effective) strategy for teaching a child to swallow a pill: Ask her to place the pill on the tip of her tongue, then give her a drink to sip with a straw. Most kids will swallow the pill without a glitch.

IF YOUR CHILD RESISTS TAKING MEDICINE

- Ask the physician why he's prescribed medication, because being firm is easier if you're well informed.
- Stay calm. It will promote confidence and help your child relax.
- Realize that your child isn't trying to be difficult on purpose.

Respond with respect. When a parent is fighting with a child about medication, he's often thinking something along the lines of "Why are you doing this to me?" He interprets the child's behavior as a personal insult and looks at it from his own perspective: "I don't have time for this silliness" or "I'm in no mood for childishness." A parent may be overly empathetic and project her own emotions onto the situation: "Poor little Timmy. He's afraid." Remember that your child is a separate person with his own fears and anxieties. By viewing your child as the owner of the problem, you will give him the respect he deserves and the encouragement he needs. Begin by telling your child, even a preverbal one, why he needs medicine and how it will help him. Assume that on some level he will understand, maybe not the words but at least the intent.

THINK IT THROUGH

Reframe

Have a heart-to-heart with yourself and ask, "How am I managing my child's resistance to taking medicine?"

Reflect

Write a description of what happens when you and your child fight about taking medicine.

_____

_____

Now write the same scenario from your child's viewpoint— as if your child is telling the story.

_____

_____

Resolve

How can I turn my child's resistance around?

_____

_____

Based on what I know about my child's nature, what will be most likely to work?

_____

HINT: If you don't solve the problem at once, don't give up. Expect your child to take a minimum of eight attempts before he catches on and takes medicine without a fuss.

Red Alert: Realistically some kids will resist taking medicine, no matter what. In which case, a gentle but firm approach is best.

MESSY BEDROOMS
Less Mess—Less Stress

I used to make a big deal about the mess in my son's bedroom," my best friend reminded me. "We'd fight about it almost every day. Then he grew up and went to university in another province and got a job on the other side of the country and moved away to another city. Now his bedroom is spotless and I can't walk past it without regret."

Keeping things in perspective may help, but it doesn't solve the problem. I, too, have argued, bickered, and battled about my kids' messes a great deal more than I'd like to admit. I'd probably still be fighting with them except for my "tidying-up principles," which I came up with a few years ago. They help me to feel less frustrated and stressed out about the whole thing. Other parents report similar results.

My kids and I no longer fight about their bedrooms because *I* have changed. After little success with nagging, I came to see that I had basically two choices: I could continue ranting and raving to no avail, or I could use the energy I was wasting on frustration and invest it in finding a solution. I chose the second option.

Suppose your child is in the habit of leaving her clothes strewn all over the place. Rather than expending energy on anger, put it to use on working out a strategy to help your child learn to pick up after herself. Sit down with your youngster and tell her that from now on, you want her to gather her clothes off the floor each morning and put them away where they belong. Don't threaten her with what will happen if she doesn't listen, just be there each morning to remind her. There is nothing wrong with pitching in until your child is more responsible and you can taper off your involvement. Although some children are naturally more organized and tidier than others, all kids can learn to take responsibility for the messes they create.

> ◅ *A more imaginative child may generate a greater mess and need more help with organization and cleanup.*

Before you jump in and try to solve the problem, stand back and consider the following questions:

1. What's wrong with this picture? Look at how the messy room is set up and decide whether it's conducive to order. Is the room organized so the child can easily store the activities that take place in the room? Can you facilitate tidying up by reorganizing the child's room?
2. How does your child's personality factor in? For instance, my daughter Marissa is very creative, and she often has several projects going on simultaneously. My son Max hates to throw anything out, and little Madison suffers from babying because she's the youngest of four. Marissa, Max, and Madison each needed a different strategy to become and stay organized. Marissa needed more space to store ongoing projects, and she needed to stop her activities earlier to allow for cleanup time. Max needed help throwing out some of the junk he'd been collecting, and Madison needed *me* to stop babying her. It is easier to help your child to become more organized when you understand the physical and psychological contributions to the problem.

Remember To . . .

Be specific. Tell your child exactly what you would like him to do. Instead of saying, "Clean up your room," say, "Pick your clothes up off the floor."

Be realistic. Don't expect to give your kids orders, then come back and find it done. You'll be less frustrated if you make peace with the fact that things won't happen that way.

Be patient. Think in terms of baby steps. Your child will find it easier to break negative habits if she isn't overwhelmed by expectations. Focus on one change at a time, beginning with whatever bothers you the most, and move forward once your child is more self-reliant in that area.

Be there. I'll warn you in advance that you'll need to go in and out of your child's room to keep him on track, lend a hand, and direct his activities. The younger the child, the more involved you should be.

Be a little less generous. Despite your good intentions, you may be contributing to the problem if you buy your kids too many toys, cool pens, and other goodies. If this is the case, put away some of the toys or make a donation to the children's hospital in your area.

Be organized. With older kids, institute a ritual of Sunday-morning cleanup time: Without exception, every family member will spend an hour organizing and straightening up his or her room. Psychologically, it's easier when everyone works together.

Be smart. Don't let the bedroom issue become a power struggle, because your child will keep his bedroom in a mess just to "win."

Be willing. Let your child, even a very young one, be involved in decorating her room. This will encourage a greater sense of responsibility and a sense of pride in the condition of her bedroom.

"Take response-ability."

Although my kids' bedrooms may not be perfect, and they still need reminders to pick up after themselves, the tone of our interactions is constructive and loving. I can't promise you perfect results, but I guarantee you won't be totally disappointed, either!

THINK IT THROUGH

Reframe

Ask, "How can I help my kids become more responsible and organized around the house?"

Reflect

What is the cause-and-effect relationship around tidying-up issues?

_____

_____

What needs to change? _____

_____

_____

Resolve

You are the CEO of your family. Map out a plan that will encourage your team to take responsibility for assets.

_____

_____

_____

NIGHTMARES
AND NIGHT TERRORS
Doing What's Right Without a Fight

W hen my eldest son, Alec, turned four, he started having bad dreams," recalls Tom, manager of a swanky downtown restaurant. "Out of the blue, Alec began waking up around midnight and charging into our bedroom screaming, 'I had a *bad, bad, bad* dream.'"

Nightmares happen because of emotional challenges with normal everyday issues. Occasional nightmares are not a cause for concern; all kids have them sooner or later. However, by seven years of age, most kids have learned to master their fears, which means fewer nightmares.

Nonetheless, frequent nightmares mean something. Sometimes the problem is obvious, such as a new sibling, a change in day care, toilet training, or a recent move. But often there is no apparent source of stress, so pay close attention to the television programs, videos, and movies your child watches. The problem should eventually declare itself.

> *Did you know that a child is ten times more likely to have a nightmare than an adult?*

"When Should I Be Worried?"

Nightmares can sometimes be a sign of a more serious emotional problem. If your child's overall behavior has changed in any serious way, or if he's experiencing emotional, social, or educational problems, then discuss your concerns with your pediatrician.* Other markers of concern include nightmares that persist beyond the age of seven, or frequent nightmares that last more than a few months. This is particularly important if your child is experiencing daytime fears or other behavioral problems.

What to Do?

When a young child has a nightmare, she can generally be comforted with physical closeness, sympathy, and reassurance. I suggest that you take her back to her room rather than bring her into yours. This will help her to feel safe in her own space.

DON'T LET FEARS TURN INTO TRAPS

If you get into the habit of lying down with your child until he falls asleep, he will come to expect it for months, or even years, down the road.

You don't need to rush in and check every closet, under the beds, and behind the curtains in an effort to reassure your youngster. In fact, by buying in to the fears, you may be sending the message that monsters are real. Instead, let your youngster know you are there to protect her; with a firm but loving approach, help her feel safe and secure. By believing in your child's strengths, you will encourage her to believe in herself.

*For instance, a previously enthusiastic youngster who begins to fuss about going to school, cries easily, complains about tummy- or headaches, and loses interest in extracurricular activities, is telling you—in the only way he knows how—that something is not "right."

Work on nightmares during the daytime by reassuring your child about whatever issue is causing her grief. I ask kids to use positive imagery to help them conquer their fears. If a child is having nightmares about ghosts, I tell her to think of ways she can triumph over the ghosts, the more spectacular the better.

When a child is having frequent nightmares, plan ahead. At bedtime ask your child to pick a favorite memory and ask her to think about it if she wakes up. Say, "If you wake up in the night, I want you to think about playing on the beach (or a similar calming place) and then close your eyes and go back to sleep." Encouraging a so-called transitional object, an object that provides comfort and support, such as a blanket or stuffed animal, is beneficial as it provides reassurance and a source of connection in times of stress.

Finally, know when to draw the line. Beware of fears becoming excuses for nighttime attention. I'm all for being there when your child needs reassurance and support, but not when "I'm scared" really means "I like it when you lie down with me until I fall asleep." In this situation, I'd say, "I know you're scared, but you're a tough kid and you can handle it. How about I check on you in ten minutes?"

There are many different and equally effective philosophies around dealing with nighttime sleep problems. So, if what you're doing is working for you, then there's no reason to change.

Night Terrors—"What's Wrong with Max?"

Max began having night terrors around five years of age, soon after we moved into our new home. He'd wake up in the middle of the night screaming, with his eyes wide open yet unseeing. He'd scream and appear agitated. But when I'd try to comfort him, he'd become combative. Knowing how to differentiate between nightmares and night terrors is essential because they're best handled differently. The following chart will help you distinguish one from the other.

NIGHT TERRORS AND NIGHTMARES

Night Terrors	Nightmares
Occur within the first few hours of sleep	Occur toward the end of the night
Child has no bad dream to report	Child has a bad dream to report
Child doesn't seem to recognize you	Child recognizes you without delay
Child won't allow you to comfort him	Child seeks comfort
Child not fully awake when he cries out	Child totally awake when he cries out
Cry may sound weird	Cry is familiar
Child behaves strangely	Child is coherent but agitated
Child has no recall of events	Child is aware of a bad dream
Child cries out during night terror	Child calls to you after nightmare
Child returns to sleep	Child reluctant to go back to bed

"That's Normal?"

A child with a night terror appears very agitated and distressed but returns to sleep easily. By the time I saw four-year-old Melinda and her lovely parents, they had already made three midnight runs to the emergency room, were seen by three different doctors, and Melinda was scheduled for an abdominal ultrasound the next day. "Melinda wakes up out of her sleep, charges downstairs, and cries about her tummy," recalls her mother. "I thought she had terrible stomach cramps, but the next morning she'd say nothing hurt." Melinda's behavior was the result of night terrors, not tummy aches. How did I know? Because Melinda had no memory of the event, it happened like clockwork, and her parents described her behavior as crazed.

The best way to deal with a night terror is to encourage the youngster back to sleep as quickly as possible. Unless your child is awake and asking for you, resist the urge to intervene. Afterward, your child will quickly return to sleep and have no memory of the event in the morning. With a better understanding of nightmares and night terrors, you will be able to handle each situation in a manner that comforts and reassures your little one and promotes good sleep habits.

Take "response-ability."
Although we have no control over a child's bad dream, we do have control over bad habits. The key is to respond to your child's needs without creating new ones.

THINK IT THROUGH

Reframe

Take inventory: "How am I handling my child's nightmares or night terrors? Am I responding in a way that contributes to or maintains sleep-related problems?"

Reflect

Evaluate your way of reacting to your child when he has a nighttime problem. How is this helping (or hurting) the situation? _____

_____

_____

Why do you respond in this manner? _____

_____

_____

I believe my child is _____

_____

_____

I respond the way I do because I feel _____

_____

_____

Describe the impact of how you respond to your child's night problems. _____

_____

_____

_____

_____

Resolve

Realize and accept that straightening out the problem isn't about straightening out the child. In the future, I plan to

_____

_____

_____

Map out a step-by-step strategy on how you will carry out these goals.

_____

_____

_____

_____

_____

TIP: Think in terms of weaning yourself out of any ineffective habits.

OVERWEIGHT KIDS AND UNDERLYING ISSUES
What Helps—What Hurts

Fat kids put up with a lot of abuse. If you're the parent of a child who's even slightly overweight, you know what I'm talking about. Excessive teasing, verbal attacks, pranks, name-calling, and rejection are painful realities for chubby youngsters.

Some parents feel powerless and frustrated with their kids' eating habits. Just yesterday Jill, the mother of an extremely overweight five-year-old boy, told me that she was planning to put a lock on the fridge door because of her son's lack of willpower. Thank goodness, I was able to talk her out of it! When I think about all the teasing that these kids are subject to, I understand why they are intolerant of any criticism, even constructive. I never discuss weight directly with kids. If parents have a weight-related concern, I prefer to meet with them alone.

> *Not infrequently, a parent thinks a child has a weight problem, but when I plot out her height and weight on a growth chart, I discover she's normal. The first step in treating obesity is to clarify whether or not it exists.*

During my residency, I subspecialized in adolescent medicine, with a special focus on teens with eating disorders. What was amazing was that in each case, an innocent remark about a child's weight triggered dieting. I developed a habit of avoiding discussions about trimming down in front of kids. The first thing I tell parents—even parents of very overweight kids—is "She doesn't need a diet, she needs healthy eating and exercise habits." Then I suggest they make changes to the family's lifestyle as a whole. Indeed, I suggest they make it a family mission.

> ⇥ *Children under the age of three should not follow any weight-loss plans; they need adequate fat in their diet for growth and brain development.*

Learn from toddlers. I'm always asking parents to notice a toddler's eating habits—she eats when she's hungry and stops when she's full. What do you think happens when a well-meaning adult decides her little one is not eating enough and prods her to eat everything on her plate, or spoon-feeds her anything left over? Or lectures her about eating more vegetables or fruits? Or sneaks bits of food into her mouth while she's playing? When a toddler stops listening to her body and eats to please her parents, she risks obesity. The moral of the story is: Your toddler knows more about what she needs to eat than you think.

Less is more. Use a plate that's one size smaller to help cut down on portions.

Fat and sugar savvy. Learn to cook with less fat and sugar, which can be done without noticeably altering the taste.

Use common sense. Obviously, making healthy choices is harder if the cupboards are full of junk. So, decrease the sweets while increasing the healthier foods in your pantry. Encourage your kids to eat veggies by topping them with colored sprinkles; the added calories are negligible, while the benefits are significant.

Give choices. Keep a variety of healthy treats in your fridge and allow your kids to choose snacks on their own.

Don't ban junk food. If you forbid junk food or nag about candy, your kids are more likely to overeat these foods when you aren't around. I noticed this phenomenon the summer I worked as a doctor at an overnight camp. Kids were weighed at the start and finish of the summer. I asked the kids who put on the most weight if they were eating differently than at home. Each child's answer was the same: "I'm not allowed to eat candy at home."

Limit juice. Kids love juice and typically drink more than you realize. The average child should be limited to six ounces of juice per day. If cutting down is a struggle, try diluting the juice—one part juice and three parts water. Water is the ideal first choice. I find kids drink more if they're given water in a sports bottle.

Don't use food as a bribe. Comments like "If you're a good girl, I'll buy you an ice cream" put an emotional value on sweets and teach kids to feed their emotions.

Minimize milk fat. Use low-fat milk or nonfat milk after the age of three. Make the switch early and you'll encounter less resistance. *Hint:* Kids need only two to three glasses of milk a day.

No snacking in front of the television. Make this a nonnegotiable rule in your home, and your kids will cut down on snacking. Better yet, if your child has a television in his room, move it. Your child's activity level will increase.

Limit television, computer, and video-game time. It's up to you to establish television rules. I recommend that television time should not exceed time spent on physical activity. If your kids play basketball for half an hour, they can watch a half-hour television program.

Don't tolerate teasing. The psychological toll on overweight kids is enormous. If your child is being teased, it is appropriate to step in on her behalf. Speak to teachers, coaches, and parents and engage their support.

Become more active. Inactivity is a major contributor to weight problems. For starters, get your child involved in sports or dance; a school gym program is not adequate exercise on its own. Also, getting active as a family will set a good example for your child.

Ban boredom eating. One of the most common habits of chubby kids is snacking when there is nothing to do. Set limits on how much your kids eat in much the same way you establish boundaries in other areas. Don't feel guilty, because your child will benefit both emotionally and physically.

Take "response-ability."

It's not a coincidence that many overweight parents have kids with weight problems. Take an honest look at your eating and exercise habits; double standards won't fly. Realistically, a healthy lifestyle will pay off not only for your child but for you, too! Use the three R's to size up your ability to help your child pare down.

THINK IT THROUGH

Reframe

Take stock: "What effect do I have on my child's eating habits?"

Reflect

Write a brief description of how you handled a recent food conflict. _____

_____

_____
_____
_____
_____
_____

How did your child respond? _____
_____

Rank the issues that are causing you grief from highest to lowest.

Setting a good example_____

Negative comments_____

Nagging_____

Cooking low-fat style_____

Saying no _____

Personal activity level _____

The family's activity level _____

Resolve

The following exercises are designed to give you practice in trading in a knee-jerk response for a mindful one.

Your son reaches for his fourth piece of pizza.

Your knee-jerk response is _____
_____

But you rise above this response and say _____
_____

It's been an hour since dinner, and your son is complaining he's hungry.

Your knee-jerk reaction is _____
_____

But you rise above this response and say _____
_____

Your daughter comes home from school crying because kids are teasing her about her weight.

Your knee-jerk reaction is _____
_____

But you rise above this response and say _____
_____

Your son is acting up in the waiting room at the doctor's office. You ask him to settle down. He asks, "Will you take me to McDonald's if I behave?"

Your knee-jerk reaction is _____
_____

But you rise above this response and say _____
_____

Your daughter does not eat everything on her plate.

Your knee-jerk response is _____
_____

But you rise above this response and say _____
_____

PICKY EATERS
No More Food Battles

Beginning around two years of age, Jackie refused to eat anything but applesauce, chicken nuggets, and bananas, all in minuscule amounts. Every meal was a major production, recalls her mother, Mandy: "I coaxed, bribed, threatened, and lectured Jackie to eat, eat, eat. But the harder I pushed, the more she resisted."

I hate fish. The more my husband pushes me to eat it—"It's good for you; it's low in fat; you'll set a good example for the kids"—the less likely I am to do so. His perfect logic does not alter the basic fact that I hate fish. The same thing happens when well-meaning grown-ups pressure kids by saying, "Kids are starving in India" or "You can't have any dessert unless you eat all your vegetables." A child who is bullied to eat will most likely respond with resistance, anger, guilt, and anxiety. Misinformation and inappropriate expectations can sabotage even the most laid-back parents.

FOOD MYTHS

Myth

A child who doesn't eat all the food groups at each meal will get sick.

Fact

In twenty-odd years as a medical doctor, I've never seen an otherwise healthy child develop health problems as a result of picky eating.

· · ·

Myth

A child who doesn't eat well should be given extra milk.

Fact

Let your child (two years and older) drink unlimited water, and keep milk to no more than four ounces at each meal (twelve ounces per day).

· · ·

Myth

A child who doesn't eat well should be spoon-fed.

Fact

Children who are spoon-fed after age two years are being taught to ignore important messages their body sends them about fullness (the same messages overeaters are encouraged to recognize and respect).

· · ·

Myth

A child who doesn't eat well needs extra snacks.

Fact

Kids need to eat about every three hours, which means your kids need a few snacks each day. Provide nutritious snacks and you won't need to worry if your child eats less at mealtime.

· · ·

Myth

A child should be expected to eat what's on his plate.

Fact

Respect your child's right to refuse certain foods, otherwise you run the risk of turning him off eating altogether.

· · ·

Myth

A child who doesn't eat well should be pressured to eat more.

Fact

Did you know that a child's stomach is about the size of your fist? Realistically, a toddler's portion should be about one fourth the size of an adult's.

· · ·

Myth

A child who doesn't eat well should be accommodated.

Fact

Respect your child's preferences, but don't feel you need to prepare separate meals to meet everyone's preferences. Teach your child early on how to make a sandwich, so he can prepare one if he doesn't want to eat what's offered.

"He Won't Eat Anything"

Mimi and Ken have a four-year-old son, Mark, who eats like a bird. "Mealtimes are horrible," lamented Mimi. "All we do is fight." According to Mark's parents, they had tried everything. "Why do you think Mark is finicky about what he eats?" I asked. Both parents looked at each other and shrugged. "Maybe we push too hard," Mimi said. "But if we don't, he won't eat anything."

We applied the three R's, and Mimi and Ken reframed the problem by asking, "How are we caught up in Mark's picky eating habits?" In Oprah's words, Mimi had an "aha" moment. She blurted out, "Do you think I monitor what Mark eats too closely? I guess I nag him about his eating habits." Indeed, the harder Mimi pushed, the more resistant little Mark became.

In this case, old habits needed to fade away before any forward movement would happen. Mimi and Ken decided that for the next few weeks, they wouldn't say a word about what Mark ate or left untouched. I had warned the couple to expect Mark to eat less initially. Human beings have a natural tendency to resist change, so Mark's behavior would likely get worse before it got better as he tried to lure his parents back into a fight. Right on cue, Mark refused to eat dinner. Neither parent said a word. Mark asked, "Do I have to eat everything on my plate?" Mimi said, "Not tonight. Just eat what you want." Mark answered, "I don't want anything." It was like he was trying to say, "Hey, you guys, you're supposed to yell at me if I don't eat." But his parents refused to bite. Once Mimi and Ken stopped worrying about Mark's eating habits, he gradually began to eat a wider range of food, and mealtime gradually became more pleasant.

"But She'll Starve"

Five-year-old Jill sits down at the dinner table and says straight-away, "I'm not eating this. I hate spaghetti." Typically, you'd say, "How about a peanut butter sandwich?" but you're tired of being a short-order cook. What do you do?

Don't

Pit yourself against your child.
"Eat your dinner or no dessert."

Do

Remember your child doesn't like tomato sauce on her spaghetti. Say, *"I know what to do,"* and give her a serving of spaghetti with the tomato sauce on the side.

Don't

Use logic.
"If you don't eat your dinner, you'll be hungry."

Do

Bite your tongue. Refuse to say anything about what she eats. Turn the conversation around by saying, *"What did you do that was fun today?"*

Don't

Resort to guilt tactics.
"You're lucky to have something to eat. Children are starving in India."

Do

Give your child a big serving of mashed potatoes (her favorite food) and a small serving of spaghetti, then say nothing about what she eats.

"I Give Him Whatever He Wants"

It's seven-thirty A.M. You have to be at work in an hour. Your four-year-old son, Luke, wants cereal for breakfast. (Great! You'll get out in time.) You place a bowl of his favorite cereal in front of him. "I want the cereal with marshmallows," cries Luke. You say, "But this is your favorite cereal." (You're out of the cereal he wants.) He screams, "I want the cereal with marshmallows!" What should you do?

Don't

Give Luke an ultimatum.
"Eat what I give you or do without breakfast."

Do

Ask yourself, "How can I solve this without a fight?" Offer alternatives? Give Luke choices? Tell him he can have the marshmallow cereal later, as a snack?

. . .

Don't

Resort to guilt tactics.
"Why can't you just eat what I give you like your brother?"

Do

Suggest another option. Luke knows how to make a peanut butter and jam sandwich.
"Here's some bread and peanut butter. Why don't you make yourself a sandwich?"

. . .

> **Don't**
>
> Try bribery.
> *"If you eat your cereal, I'll give you a treat for a snack."*
>
> **Do**
>
> Recognize and accept that your child isn't a morning person.
> *"How about a piece of toast instead?"*

Take "response-ability."

Employ the three R's to help overcome the impulse to push your little one to eat. Invest that energy in creating relaxed mealtime experiences. A peaceful atmosphere is more likely to help your child develop an appreciation for food and family.

> ## THINK IT THROUGH
>
> **Reframe**
>
> Ask, "How am I involved in food battles?"
>
> **Reflect**
>
> Understanding your contribution to a problem is an essential step toward resolving it.
>
> What distresses you about your child's eating habits?
>
> _____
>
> Who is most concerned about your child's eating habits?
>
> _____

Are your worries valid? Does your doctor agree that your child's eating habits need to change?

_____

Are your perceptions of how much food your child needs possibly wrong?_____

_____

What influence has pressuring your child had on his eating habits?_____

_____

Exactly what is it you fear will happen as a result of your child's eating habits? _____

_____

What do you think your child feels, thinks, or perceives when pressure is on him to eat? _____

_____

If I asked your child how he feels when Mommy or Daddy says he needs to eat more vegetables (or other healthy food), what would he say? _____

_____

_____

Resolve

Rank the reasons food battles are happening from most to least likely.

• My child is using food as a power trip.

_____

• My youngster is hypersensitive to taste and texture.

_____

• In-laws put pressure on me to make my child eat more.

_____

- My perceptions of how much food my child needs may be wrong.

  _____

- Not eating has turned into a power struggle between my child and me.

  _____

- I am a worrier.

  _____

Write a brief comment about how you can work on each of the issues that pertain to you.

_____

_____

_____

RED ALERT: Do you really want to be fighting about food for the next month, year, or longer? The patterns you establish now will continue until you take active steps to change them.

Map out a seven-day strategy to reshape your interactions around food.

Monday _____

Tuesday _____

Wednesday _____

Thursday _____

Friday _____

Saturday _____

Sunday _____

POUTING
Dos and Don'ts

"Mommy, can we bake cookies?" asks four-year-old Sara. Her mother, Tracy, sole owner of a family engraving company, says, "No, I've got too much work to do." Sara stamps her feet and says, "You're mean. I never get to do anything." For the next half hour, Sara follows her mother around wearing an "oh poor me" face. Tracy is determined not to let Sara's dramatics get to her, but they do. Call it passive aggressive, manipulative, or guiltmongering—to be sure, pouting works like a charm. The following list of dos and don'ts will help you manage pouting and simultaneously teach your child how to handle disappointment with grace and dignity.

DO talk about feelings. By acknowledging your child's disappointment, you help him recognize and express his feelings. If your child complains when it's time to leave a friend's home, say, "I know you're disappointed that we have to go home now, but it's time to go." Children need to know that what they feel matters. But they don't need to get their way.

DON'T be overly permissive. When a little tyke associates being loved with getting his way, he won't take no for an answer.

DO give choices. When children feel powerless about the events in their life, they resort to passive-aggressive ways of expressing themselves, such as pouting, whining, and complaining. You can help your child feel in control by giving him plenty of room to make decisions. When Sara, mother of two, tells her children they can't do something, she gives them other options: "No, you can't watch television, but how about you and I whip up some cookies?"

DON'T spoil your kids. Even if you could afford to buy every gadget on the toy shelves, it would not be in your child's best interest to do so. A spoiled child is more likely to have problems with peers and in other relationships because he lacks experience in compromising and managing frustration.

DO encourage gratitude. Teach your kids to focus on the good things in their lives by seeing the cup as half full, not half empty. Make appreciation a part of daily conversation: "What's the best thing that happened at school today?" "What did you do that was fun today?" "Name two things that made you feel happy today." As with everything else about raising children, living by example is the most powerful lesson. Give children positive examples about how to enjoy life as it is, rather than complaining about all that it is not.

DON'T raise your kids on guilt. If you use guilt as a tactic to motivate your children, be prepared for it to be used right back on you. Your kids will say things like "You never let me stay up late." "Thanks a lot for forgetting to buy the chocolate milk you promised." "Why can't I have a friend sleep over . . . Madison always gets to have a sleepovers." "You never help me anyway." "You care more about your book than you do about me." Raise kids without guilt by making a commitment to doing so. The following are examples of how we (unwittingly) foster guilt:

- By referring to our child's past mistakes
- By comparing a child with siblings or friends
- By the language we use: "Why don't you ever listen?" "What's the matter with you?" "What do you think your grandfather would say if he knew what you did?" "Swear to God?"

DO look for solutions, not faults. When children are taught to focus on solutions instead of faults, they grow up with a sense of responsibility and learn how to remedy a situation rather than waste time and energy complaining about it.

If Your Child Says

"I never get to do anything fun."

She's Feeling

"I feel frustrated."

Don't Say

"That's not true. I took you to the playground yesterday."

Instead, Say

"I'd love to read you a book. Why don't you go and pick one out, and we'll read it as soon as I've finished what I'm doing."

• • •

If Your Child Says

"It's not fair. I never get to stay up late, but Benjamin gets to do everything . . . you love him more. You're mean."

She's Feeling

"I feel left out."

Don't Say

"I love you both the same."

Instead, Say

"You sound very upset. When you cool off, I'd like to talk about it."

• • •

If Your Child Says

"I'm not going to talk to you ever again."

She's Feeling

"I'm going to make you feel guilty for saying no to me."

Don't Say

"Stop acting like a spoiled brat."

Instead, Say

"Let's talk when you've calmed down."

. . .

If Your Child Says

"Why do I have to go to Sunday school?"

She's Feeling

"It isn't fair."

Don't Say

"Because I said so, that's why."

Instead, Say

"What's the problem with Sunday school? Tell me so I can help you fix it."

. . .

If Your Child Says

"I don't want to go on the class trip."

She's Feeling

"I'm scared."

Don't Say

"What's the matter with you? The trip will be fun."

Instead, Say

"Why not? Let's talk about it."

≫ *A child who is worried will complain: "I don't want to go to the party." "Why do I have to go swimming?" "I hate gymnastics." By talking with your kids, you can differentiate between worrying and pouting. Ask open-ended questions like "Why don't you want to go to the party?" "What is it about swimming that you don't like?"*

Take "response-ability."

Pouting is only as effective as you allow it to be. You can't force your child to stop pouting, but you can stop yourself from reacting to it. If a youngster doesn't get the kind of reaction he's looking for, he'll stop.

THINK IT THROUGH

Reframe

Consider: "How do I foster pouting?" Become an anthropologist studying you. This means attempting to understand your own behavior, thoughts, and feelings without being judgmental.

Reflect

Think in fifty-fifty terms: You each contribute equally to the dynamic between you.

_____

My youngster pouts and I

_____

_____

He counterreacts by

_____

_____

_____

Resolve

Remedy the problem by changing how you respond to it. Map out a plan to solve the problem.

_____

_____

_____

TIP: Just because your child pouts doesn't mean you need to respond to it. He's entitled to his feelings, but you don't need to endorse them.

POWER STRUGGLES
Make Peace, Not War

Three-and-a-half-year-old Molly had always been a low-maintenance child, so her mother, Annie, was taken completely by surprise when power struggles appeared out of nowhere. If Molly was asked to put away her toys, she'd put her hands on her hips, stamp her feet, and shout, *"No!"* If Molly was told it was bath time, she'd run away. Annie tried reasoning with Molly, giving her choices and using positive reinforcement, but nothing worked. Molly was becoming more rebellious each day, and the power struggles were becoming more difficult to tolerate.

What's the best defense against a power struggle? Knowing how to avoid one altogether. Parents sometimes get caught up in power struggles because they think they need to teach little Johnny "who's the boss." Some parents want to prove to themselves that they can force a youngster to back down. And others think it's for a child's own good: *Kids need to learn respect.* But realistically, the only thing a power struggle teaches a youngster is how to be defiant, stubborn, and angry. Avoiding power struggles is quite simple if you adhere to these three fundamental principles:

1. *Be flexible*. With creative thinking, you can come up with solutions that are peaceful and mutually acceptable. Let's think about the toddler who runs away from her bath. Mom has two choices: 1) She can get huffy and say, "You've got till the count of three to get into this bath," or 2) she can get smart and say, "Let's see if you can find six yellow toys for the bath." Most kids will rise to the challenge.

2. *Be respectful.* The key ingredient to cooperation is remembering that your child is a person. Do you feel angry when someone orders you around? If someone refused to listen to what you had to say, wouldn't you feel hurt? Children are no different. Parents make demands, sometimes completely unreasonable ones, and become annoyed if the child doesn't immediately obey. "I asked you to sit quietly" and "Do as you're told" are inflammatory comments and not likely to inspire cooperation. Parents must become more mindful about what they say and how they say it.

3. *Be a team player.* Two minds are better than one. Asking your child, "What would you like to do while I talk to Doctor C.?" will motivate her to behave; comments like "I asked you to sit down. Now do as you're told!" will cause a rebellion.

CHANCES ARE, YOU'LL HAVE PROBLEMS IF YOU . . .

- Make demands when your child is tired or grumpy, or if you deal with a problem when you're stressed or worn out.
- Bribe your child to behave. This teaches him to behave if, and only if, he is rewarded.
- Label your child. This emphasizes negative qualities, and when we focus on problems, troubles escalate.

"But He Won't Listen to Me"

Not all power struggles can be avoided, because defiance is a natural part of a child's struggle for independence and autonomy. However, knowing how to respond to your child's oppositional behavior will help you prevent antagonism and restore harmony. First, it's up to you to drop out of power struggles. While it takes two people to keep a showdown alive, it takes only one to end it, and since you're the adult, it's up to you to do so.

What not to do. Don't dig in your heels and insist your child do as he's told. He is less likely to be flexible if you respond to his misbehavior with anger. According to a recent study done by the National Institute of Mental Health, children of mothers who overreact to bad behavior are more likely to have discipline problems.

> *You can't encourage cooperation if you're competing for control.*

What to do. There are many ways, all equally effective, to drop out of power struggles. My favorite is to say, "We're both angry now. Why don't we talk about it later?" Another strategy is to identify with your child: "I know just how you feel. Sometimes I hate brushing my teeth, too." Then try to solve your problem using teamwork. Ask yourself, "How can I foster cooperation?" and you'll both come out winners.

What not to do. Don't spank your child. It may solve your problems for the moment, but it will increase them down the road. Don't yell. Yelling may solve the problem temporarily, but kids raised on yelling eventually become parent-deaf.

What to do. The key to dealing with a defiant child is not to come across as demanding, pushy, or bossy. Rather, try to understand your child's perspective, and then invite him to cooperate: "I've got a problem—I want you to wear a hat because I'm worried you'll catch a cold. But you hate wearing anything on your head. What should we do?" A youngster is more likely to compromise if he's involved in finding a solution.

Who's the Boss?

You ask your five-year-old daughter, Lisa, to sit quietly and stop making so much noise so you can speak with the doctor. She ignores you. You ask her a second time. She stamps her foot and says, "No!" By now you're totally embarrassed. How do you handle this situation?

Don't

Issue another warning.
"Sit down. I don't like how you're behaving."

Do

Calm yourself before speaking.
"Can you think of something quiet to do while I'm talking to the doctor?"

. . .

Don't

Spank your child's bottom.
"Do as you're told."

Do

Try to understand why your child is misbehaving. She most likely feels left out, so say,
"Would you like to sit on my lap while I chat with the doctor?"

. . .

> **Don't**
>
> Offer a bribe.
> *"If you're quiet, I'll buy you a toy."*
>
> **Do**
>
> Be realistic about your child's ability to sit quietly.
> *"Do you want to draw? I brought your favorite crayons along."*

"Read My Lips"

You tell your four-year-old that it's bedtime, and she promptly runs away. You give her a warning: "If you're not in bed by the count of three, you won't be allowed to watch any television tomorrow night." You count to three and she doesn't budge. What now?

> **Don't**
>
> Yell louder.
> *"I'm losing my patience."*
>
> **Do**
>
> Ask your child to help you solve the problem.
> *"Gosh, Megan, I have a problem. I want you to go to bed now, and you want to stay up. How should we solve this problem?"*
>
> • • •

Don't

Try reasoning.
"If you don't go to bed now, you'll be tired tomorrow."

Do

Focus on getting your small fry to bed without a fight.
"Come and pick out the book we're going to read tonight."

•   •   •

Don't

Give up.
"Okay, just put yourself to bed when you're ready."

Do

Give directions, not demands.
"Now we're going to go upstairs and get ready for bed."

What to Do When Nothing Works

Defer the problem. You can say, "I'm too upset to deal with this now. Let's both cool down and talk about it later."

Agree with your child. "You're right. Eight-thirty is too early for your bedtime. From now on, you can stay up till eight thirty-five." (It doesn't hurt to let your child feel like a winner every once in a while.)

Distract him. Say, "It's lunchtime. Come and sit down and we'll talk about it later."

Call a truce. Say, "Let's agree to disagree on this one."

Ask your child for his input. Say, "Can you help me solve this problem?"

Take "response-ability."

Let us face one final fact: It takes two to tango. Power struggles don't happen without a parent's full participation. Here's where employing the three R's can help you become more conscious and less reactive. As you begin to shed light on your role, you'll figure out precisely how to solve problems without bruising relationships.

THINK IT THROUGH

Reframe

Begin by asking yourself, "How am I contributing to power struggles?"

Reflect

Understand what you're doing that has allowed the situation to get where it is now. Use the acronym S-T-O-P to help you zero in on your behavior.

See. Replay a situation in your mind that is causing you grief. Focus on how you managed a particular adversarial situation and think about your child's counteraction. _____

_____

Think. How does my thinking influence the way I respond? "I'm bigger, older, and more experienced, and my child should listen to me—end of story." _____

_____

Observe. Take a step backward and notice your body language, tone of voice, and facial expressions. Try to remember how you felt as a child when your parents or teachers reprimanded you. _____

_____

Put it together. How do your mental and emotional contributions influence your knee-jerk reactions?

_____

_____

_____

_____

Resolve

Think in very precise terms about what you can do to redirect your child's behavior.

I ask my six-year-old to come to the table and he says, "Later."

My knee-jerk reaction is

_____

_____

But I stop myself and instead I

_____

_____

You ask your child to clean up and he just keeps on playing as if he didn't hear you.
My knee-jerk response is

_____

_____

But I stop myself and instead I

_____

_____

You want your child to wear a sweater because it's cold outside, but he refuses.

My knee-jerk reaction is

_____

_____

But I stop myself and instead I

_____

_____

RED ALERT: Stop and think before you respond to your child's misbehavior. Choose actions with positive consequences.

QUARRELS
Conflict Resolution Skills
(Beginner's Version)

One night many years ago, as I lay in bed listening to my kids fighting in the next room, I realized something amazing. My children were pros at antagonizing and tormenting one another, but they didn't have a clue when it came to resolving differences. How had I not seen it before? They knew exactly how to push one another's buttons, get on one another's nerves, hurt one another's feelings, and make one another cry. But they didn't know how to make peace. That was my job. When I couldn't stand the fighting anymore, I'd barge in and take over. But what kind of lesson was I teaching my kids—that they couldn't figure things out without me? That they didn't even need to try? After coming to the conclusion that there will always be differences, I decided to teach my kids the skills needed to end them. Are kids capable of damage control? Not only are they capable, even the very young can act as her own "consultant."

The process. Sit down with your kids at a time when everyone is getting along, and establish some ground rules. For instance, say, "From now on, when you kids are fighting, I'm going to ask you to put your fight on hold and come together to solve the problem." The following acronym—W-I-N-S—will help you guide your kids in the art of negotiation. The idea is to use this strategy when kids are "stuck" in fighting mode and you want to redirect their focus.

Work together. Each child gets an opportunity to voice her opinion. The focus should be on finding solutions, not faults.

Interrupting is not allowed. Listen to each other without butting in.

No backtracking. This is not a time to bring up past complaints. Focus on the problem at hand.

Stay with negotiations. Agree to work on the problem until you reach a solution that's acceptable to all.

Once you've established guidelines, act as the mediator and facilitate discussion. Let each child offer an idea on how to solve the problem. Keep going from one child to another, giving each an opportunity to comment on the ideas and offer solutions. Keep at it until a consensus is reached. This process teaches kids how to compromise and become solution-oriented. I'm not going to pretend that your kids will never fight again; that's not going to happen. But they can learn to negotiate, and when this happens, less energy is wasted on fighting and more is left over for having fun.

Use the three R's to focus on what you can teach your kids that will help them live together more peacefully and lovingly.

THINK IT THROUGH

Reframe

Take stock: "What role do I play in bickering?"

Reflect

What do you do when the kids squabble?

How do you decide when to intervene?

_____

How do you determine who's at fault?

_____
_____
_____
_____
_____
_____

Resolve

Create a game plan to help your children become more effective problem solvers.

_____
_____
_____
_____
_____

HINT: Be patient. It will take at least a month before you see any signs of improvement.

SCHOOL PROBLEMS YOU MAY ENCOUNTER
And What You Can Do About Them

I know that the day after report cards are sent home, at least ten to fifteen parents will call my office for an urgent consultation. The mother of six-year-old Shane called because he was having problems completing his homework. Tracy's mother and father called because the teacher commented on her short attention span. And Luc's mother was worried about his behavior; apparently he was more interested in socializing than doing work. When a child is having school problems, the first thing I want to clarify is whether the child is having a *behavioral, emotional,* or *academic* problem, or all of the above. For the purposes of our discussion, we will separate the issues, although in real life they tend to overlap, at least to some degree.

Behavioral Problems

A child who is acting up at school may be doing so for many reasons. Because parents are not there to witness the problem themselves, they are dependent on teachers and other school officials to fill in the blanks. Try to get a clear picture of the situation that is causing grief without becoming defensive or angry. Hang back and consider the big picture before taking any active steps to remedy it.

How is your child doing socially? A child may become the class clown in order to gain acceptance of his peers.

What is your child gaining from this behavior? A child may act up for the entertainment of his peers or because he is having academic problems. A child with a learning disability may misbehave in order to avoid doing work, or as a result of frustration. On the other hand, a child for whom the work is too easy may disrupt others out of boredom.

How would you describe your child's temperament? A busy child may find it hard to sit still, and a spirited child may find it hard to remain quiet, while an impulsive child may find taking turns a challenge.

Are problems at home spilling over? If a child is worried about a sick parent or sibling, or if there is marital conflict, schoolwork may seem trivial.

Is your child developmentally on track with his class? Kids mature at their own speed. This can be a problem when a child is developmentally out of sync with his classmates.

Is your child on any medication (over-the-counter, prescribed, herbal, or home remedy) that interferes with her behavior? Cough medications can make kids drowsy or hyperactive. Asthma medications can make kids agitated or disruptive, and they may experience a decrease in their ability to concentrate.

Does your child's behavior reflect bigger problems? Attention deficit disorder or learning disabilities should be considered in any child who is having significant school problems.

Emotional Issues

Although we tend to think of childhood as stress-free, this assumption is unfortunately far from the truth. While children don't need to worry about getting to the office on time, they are not exempt from stress, sadness, anxiety, or depression. There's a fine line between a small dose of stress working as a motivating force and the negative impact of too much stress on learning, social ability, and overall health. Kids are coping with many complicated issues today, and while many manage without overt problems, others do not. A child who's depressed may find it hard to concentrate in class. A highly anxious child may find classroom participation impossible and do poorly on tests. Poor anger management may lead to aggressiveness and fighting in the schoolyard. You need to understand a problem before you take steps to solve it.

Is my child the target of bullying or teasing? Jill's mother remembers the painful time her daughter had in grade one: "She was called 'Fatso' and 'Piggy' by her classmates." The problem was complicated by Jill's increasingly difficult behavior at home. "I was preoccupied dealing with her anger outbursts, and I didn't stop and think about where it was coming from," recalls Jill's mom. "Had I known that she was being teased at school, I would have handled things differently at home."

Does my child miss too many days of school? I have known mothers who, when feeling lonely or depressed, will keep a child at home unnecessarily. If this strikes a chord, I highly recommend you do something to remedy your emotional wellness rather than using your child to feel better.

Is the teacher a good fit for my child? I will never forget Gregory, the six-year-old I was asked to treat for weight loss. He lost close to twenty pounds and spent at least a month in the hospital. After extensive investigations, all of which came back normal, Gregory disclosed that he was terrified of his teacher. While in the hospital, the "butterflies" in his stomach settled down, and he regained his weight, and then some. The teacher was not the problem; she was well liked by the other children and parents. Gregory's tale is an extreme example of how a poor child-teacher fit can impact a youngster's emotional and physical wellness.

Is the school's learning style a good match for my child's temperament? Put your personal views and philosophies about education aside and think about how your child fits into the school environment.

What is my child's mood? Are unrelated emotional problems interfering with your youngster's ability to learn?

Academic Problems

One day last week, I got a call from Cindy, mother of six-year-old Troy. She has always struck me as being laid-back, so I knew something was terribly wrong when I heard her in tears, unable to collect herself enough to talk. The night before, she and her husband were asked to come to the school to discuss Troy's school progress. "That's when they dropped the bomb," Cindy said. "His teacher thinks he has a problem." There are many reasons why a child may have difficulty learning. Some of these we've already touched on, like the child who is having difficulty concentrating because of teasing, but other causes would include hearing or vision problems, developmental lags, school absenteeism, too many extracurricular activities, intellectual causes, or learning disabilities. These are the kind of questions you should ask to tease out the problem.

Does my child have enough time to do homework or assignments? Many of today's kids are so heavily booked that they need Palm Pilots to organize their extracurricular activities.

Could my child have hearing or vision problems? Many a school problem has been solved once a child's visual or hearing problem has been identified. I would highly recommend a formal hearing and vision assessment for any child with learning problems. Last week I treated a lovely nine-year-old girl whose grades were steadily going downhill. Her speech was normal, and her mother had no concerns about her hearing. But formal testing revealed that this girl was moderately hearing-impaired and that she had learned to read lips to compensate.

Do I need to take my child to the doctor? There are a few medical conditions that can affect a child's learning ability, for instance, thyroid problems, lead ingestion, or chromosome abnormalities. However, the vast majority of the time, a learning difficulty does not indicate an underlying health problem.

How does my attitude affect my child's? This is a good time to think about your own attitudes toward school. Was your experience a positive one? One father I knew put enormous pressure on his kids to succeed; he wasn't satisfied with anything less than straight A's. He had dropped out of school at a young age and didn't want his kids to do the same. Although his concern was coming from a caring place, his impact on the children was primarily negative: One son had almost entirely stopped putting any effort into his schoolwork, figuring, "Why bother?" because his father was never satisfied.

Does my child have a learning disability? Approximately 10 percent of the North American population has a learning disability, which means a person has difficulty learning despite a normal intelligence level. Any persistent learning problem that is not explained by another cause should be formally investigated to rule out a learning disability.

Does my child have an attention problem? Some children have difficulty paying attention, which interferes with the ability to concentrate and learn. If your child has a short attention span, is inattentive, and is easily distracted—with or without behavioral problems—discuss your concerns with your pediatrician and the child's teacher.

Teacher's Pet

The ideal relationship between you, the teacher, and any other educators should be one of mutual respect and cooperation. All too often, however, I find teachers and parents pitted against each other. In the best-case scenario, teacher and parents pool their expertise and knowledge and work together to help the child. Parents can share their ideas about what works best with their kids, and teachers can ask parents for their cooperation and involvement around school issues. If the relationship with your child's teacher has gotten off on the wrong foot, go back to square one and work at getting it on track.

THINK IT THROUGH

Reframe

Evaluate: "How am I responding to my child's school problems?"

Reflect

Take a moment and consider the role you play in managing school difficulties.

_____

_____

_____

_____

_____

Which word more closely describes your guidance: "coach" or "critic"?

_____

If you answered "critic," why do you assume this approach?

_____

Resolve

Regardless of the root cause of the school problems, your child needs you as his advocate. You can do a great deal to help him once you understand the issues.

HOMEWORK: Devise a game plan to help bring out the best in your child's academic performance.

_____

_____

_____

_____

_____

SCHOOL REFUSAL
What You Should Know
and What You Should Do

Andrea, nurse coordinator of the ambulatory pediatric clinic at a large teaching hospital, has more than five years' experience working with children. Confidence and solid information are not things she lacks. So, when her five-year-old daughter fussed about going to school the first day, Andrea knew exactly what to do. What she wasn't prepared for was how awful she would feel doing it. Andrea had to peel her daughter's fingers off her sleeve, one by one, in order to break free.

"School refusal" is the medical term used to characterize a child's unwillingness to go to school, regardless of the root cause. Young kids communicate via their behavior, and a child who lacks readiness and fusses about going to school is in effect saying, "I *really* can't deal with this!" A child may refuse to go to school because he's worried about what is happening at home, particularly when parents are fighting or a family member is unwell. Another consideration is whether your child is experiencing academic or social problems. Have a chat with your child's teacher and ask the following questions: How are his grades? Does he have friends? Is he being teased or bullied? But by far, the most common reason for school refusal is separation anxiety. The child experiences distress at separating from his mother or father but afterward is worry-free. Obviously, the manner in which you resolve the problem will depend in part on the underlying cause.

The best way to avoid school refusal is to be proactive. Bring your child to school several times the year before she will attend. Take her on a tour of the school so she knows the building and doesn't feel lost on her first day. And if at all possible, try and introduce her to other youngsters who will be in the same class. The following philosophies and commonsense strategies are designed to ease separation anxiety and increase your child's sense of comfort.

Give clear messages. Your child needs to know that you expect him to attend school no matter how much he complains, cries, or makes a scene.

Keep good-byes short and sweet. Brief good-byes will convey that you have confidence in your child's ability to cope, whereas hovering will send the message "I'm worried about you."

Give Dad a turn. Whoever has the least difficulty separating from the child should be the one to drop her off. My daughter Madison made a huge fuss until my eldest daughter starting taking her to class. After months of fussing, Madison quickly settled down.

Comfort your child with memories of home. Some children like to bring something special from home—a blanket, a pillow, or a stuffed animal. A family picture can be comforting, and lunchbox notes can help create a sense of connection.

FOUR BEHAVIORS TO LOSE

The following behaviors are unlikely to help and may even make things worse:

1. Asking your child to stop fussing
2. Bribing your child to behave
3. Keeping your child at home
4. Sneaking out when your child is distracted

Use routines. Structure is comforting when life is stressful. Keep the same morning routine and your child will know what to expect. Better yet, begin this routine before the school year so your child is not faced with multiple changes at once.

Create good-bye rituals. "Kiss-hug-nose-rub-throw-a-kiss" has been our good-bye ritual from the get-go. Good-bye rituals help kids prepare for separation and make for easier good-byes.

> ❧ *Overprotective parents are more likely to find that their child has difficulty with separation. Not only does the child need to overcome his uneasiness, but he has to contend with his parents' futzing around as well. For example, when a parent comes back to check on her child after supposedly leaving, a youngster who has already settled down will start up again. Or if a parent displays her own discomfort at leaving, the child gets the message that there is something to worry about and resists even more. Worse yet, if a parent decides not to leave, and either takes the child home or stays with her, the child learns that crying works to her benefit. If you are anxious about letting your school-aged child out of your sight, then you will need to work on your own fears in order to help your little one overcome his.*

THINK IT THROUGH

Reframe

Consider: "How do I feed into my child's reluctance to go to school?"

Reflect

How do you manage your child's resistance to going to school?

_____

_____

Why do you respond in this manner?

_____

_____

What emotional baggage contributes to your way of dealing with the situation?

_____

_____

Resolve

To become "unstuck," think of other options or ways of handling good-byes.

_____

_____

_____

HINT: As your child masters her emotions, she will become a stronger person, and you will discover a new level of confidence in yourself as a parent.

SHARING
What's Reasonable—What's Not?

When my youngest was four years old, she became very possessive about her toys. Out of the blue, Madison decided that no one was allowed to touch anything that belonged to her, including her younger cousin who was visiting at the time. Here we were, three adults—my husband, my sister-in-law, and me—with more degrees than children, and among us we couldn't convince Madison to share even her least favorite toys. Worse yet, we couldn't agree on how to handle the situation. My husband told Madison in no uncertain terms, "You've got to the count of three to share with your cousin." My sister-in-law said, "It's okay. Anisette can find something else to do." And for my part, I criticized my husband by saying, "You're being unfair."

What would you do in this situation? Madison is eight now, and sharing is no longer a major issue for her. But every day I get calls from frustrated, confused, and embarrassed mothers, asking me how to deal with similar problems. How will a child learn to share? Good question. Indeed, I heard of one play group that asked a mother and her four-year-old child to leave because of a disagreement about resolving sharing issues.

> ⇥ *When I was a teenager, I wore a button that said,*
> *QUESTION AUTHORITY. While I am no longer a*
> *rebellious teenager, I continue to question much of*
> *what I hear—and so "should" you. Don't let*

> *anyone tell you what you should do. Analyze your situation, know your child, trust your instincts, and then do what you think is right.*

Typically, we overemphasize the importance of handling problems the right way while failing to appreciate the significance of setting a good example. Children learn more about generosity and fairness from how we live our day-to-day life than from any adult-imposed sharing lesson. Without realizing it, we set examples every day, and over time, each small action has an additive effect.

Imagine going to a weight-loss clinic where a grossly overweight counselor is lecturing you about changing your eating habits. Your reaction would likely be "Why should I listen to her?" So it is with your family. You can lecture your child about not sharing, you can give him time-outs for grabbing, you can yell at him about acting selfish—but to a child, the strongest lesson is an authentic one. If your goal is to teach your child to share, and you want to instill an appreciation for friendship and giving, then you must try to portray the qualities that you hope will rub off on your child.

But what about the here and now—what's a parent to do when a child refuses to share a toy with his sibling or friend? Let's answer this question by first looking at what not to do.

Never force a child. What do you think a child learns when a toy is snatched away from him and given to another child? Imagine for a moment that your boss walks into your office, grabs your laptop off your desk, then turns around and gives it to a coworker. Is there any reason to assume that this would inspire in you a desire to share? Aren't you in fact more likely to become tightfisted? You, as the most influential person in your child's life, can teach the values that lead to sharing without forcing them upon him.

> ✒ *When youngsters play together regularly, it's a good idea for mothers to discuss among themselves beforehand how they want to manage sharing conflicts.*

Don't force older kids to share with younger ones. Younger kids want to be like their older siblings. When my eldest daughter is playing with a ball, her younger brother and sister want the ball, the pen, the book, the toy, whatever it is that she's playing with. But is it fair to expect my daughter to give her younger siblings a turn just because they want one? Sometimes we forget that the flip side of sharing is respect. Teaching siblings to respect another's space is as important as the generosity of spirit we want to instill in them.

> ✒ *If siblings are fighting over a toy, most parents will intervene and tell the older child to give the toy to the younger one. But it's far better to encourage them to work it out among themselves.*

Never force kids to take turns. Taking turns is a basic strategy parents use to teach their kids to share. But a child needs to understand the concept of time before this lesson is of any instructive value. Be aware that time concepts don't develop until the age of three.

Never, ever pry a toy out of your child's hands. I can't think of a single situation, other than a safety issue, where I would say it's justified to snatch a toy from a child's hand. When you resort to physical force, you're teaching your kids to do the same. It's far better to ask for the toy and hold out your hand—most often, if you use a no-nonsense tone of voice, your child will likely cooperate. A toddler who is unwilling to give up a toy shouldn't be forced to do so—the lesson is lost if force is necessary.

When parents get involved in toy squabbles, the primary goal should not be to teach your child a lesson on sharing. Rather, the goal is to intervene in a manner that does no harm (i.e., doesn't create bad feelings between the kids). Children are highly sensitive to silent messages. If a parent asks an older sibling to hand over the toy he's playing with to his younger brother, the older child hears, "Mom likes the baby better than me." If one child whines to his mother and she gets involved on his behalf, the other child is bound to feel hurt and resentful toward his sibling. Take a commonsense approach and intervene in a manner that does no harm.

Look for solutions, not faults. If kids are fighting over a toy and they can't find a solution, hold both children responsible for the conflict and encourage them to work it out between themselves. The trick is to give the kids the tools they need to resolve these conflicts, then stay out of things as much as possible. One tool that works well is to say, "Okay, we've got a problem. Both of you want to play with the same toy, and that's not possible. How can we solve this problem?" Then stand back and let your kids work it out. Another strategy is to give your children a few options and let them choose.

Be realistic. By the very nature of how a child develops a sense of himself and the world around him, selfishness precedes generosity. When you recognize that this is a normal part of infant development, responding calmly and compassionately to squabbles will become easier.

> ❧ *If your child is refusing to share, avoid bribing him to do so. Bribery may buy you a few moments of peace, but in the long run, it teaches your child not to share until he's offered something in return.*

Apologize on your toddler's behalf. If your toddler grabs a toy from another child, there's nothing wrong with apologizing on your child's behalf. In this way, you show the other child respect without harboring unrealistic expectations of your little one.

Observe without intervention. When your children are fighting over a toy, resist the urge to jump into the ring along with them (unless, of course, things are getting physical). This behavior leads to win-lose outcomes, which often means someone's going to get hurt. In addition, your children will learn to depend on you to solve their problems.

Know yourself. Sandy, whose toddler doesn't object when a toy is grabbed out of her hand, can't tolerate her daughter's timidity, so she jumps in. "Excuse me, Jenny is playing with that toy," she says, as she thinks, "Oh, poor Jenny." Then she insists that the other child return the toy. One day it occurred to Sandy that it didn't bother Jenny when someone took a toy out of her hand. She realized that she was reacting to her own feelings about the situation and ignoring her daughter's reactions. After this epiphany, she stopped stepping in on her daughter's behalf. What's important is to stop projecting our own emotions onto a situation. Ask yourself, "Who owns the problem?"

> ❧ *When you solve your child's problems for her, she learns to mistrust her own abilities and fails to develop the skills or confidence level she needs to become more independent.*

Use distraction. You can turn your child's mood around by getting him involved in something different. Not every toy conflict needs to become a platform for teaching your child about sharing.

Don't add fuel to the fire. Jack wants his sister's coloring book, which she has no intention of sharing. Is it essential that the kids take turns? No, what's essential is this: Don't increase sibling rivalry by putting yourself between the kids.

Understand sibling dynamics. A youngster may be generous with friends but unwilling to share with a sibling because he's busy keeping score. "You wouldn't let me look at your loot bag—so why should I give you a piece of gum?" A scorecard mentality leads to resentment, bitterness, and grudges. Break this habit by helping your kids see the things they do for each other, instead of obsessing about the things they don't. A simple comment like "That was nice of your brother to lend you his skates" is sometimes all that's needed.

> ❧ *One family I know encourages their kids to share the limelight. Every Sunday night, they have a family concert; one child plays the piano, another tells jokes, and the youngest reads to show off her new skills.*

Work on relationships. Sometimes the problem lies in the relationship. Are you likely to share with someone you're angry with? Would you give up something you cherish to someone whom you resent? Unlikely. Try to resolve some of the deeper issues present in your child's reactions.

Acknowledge generosity. When I came down for breakfast one morning, I found my son Max preparing treats for all of his friends at school. When I saw what he was doing, I almost blurted out, "I need to feed your whole class?" I caught myself, and instead of criticizing him, I praised him for being a good friend.

Take "response-ability."

Sure, it's embarrassing when kids are inconsiderate or greedy, but when you have confidence in your child's basic goodwill, you're less apt to feel angry or frustrated and better able to respond to conflicts with gentle understanding.

THINK IT THROUGH

Reframe

Clarify: "How am I influencing my child's attitudes around sharing?"

Reflect

Use the acronym S-T-O-P to understand your end of the equation.

See. Replay in your mind the situation that is causing you grief.

_____

Think. How does my thinking influence the situation?

_____

Observe. Take a step backward and notice your body language, tone of voice, and facial expressions.

_____

Put it together. How do your mental and emotional contributions influence your knee-jerk reactions?

_____

Resolve

Let's practice exchanging a knee-jerk response for a mindful one.

Your four-year-old snatches the rattle away from the baby. Your knee-jerk reaction is

_____

But you stop yourself and instead you

_____

Your five-year-old refuses to give her little sister a turn on the swing.

Your knee-jerk reaction is

_____

But you stop yourself and instead you

_____

The baby of the family wants a turn, and the older kids are refusing to share.

Your knee-jerk reaction is

_____

But you stop yourself and instead you

_____

SHOPPING DISCIPLINE
Getting It Done Without Getting Undone

Why don't kids behave in the supermarket? Is it hopeless to expect more? Why do they want us to buy them everything in sight? "Am I doomed to be one of those mothers who scream at their kids in the mall?" Parents frequently ask me about their kid's public misbehavior and complain that shopping trips are a nightmare. But have you ever stopped to wonder why?

Here's the dilemma in a nutshell: Our goals and the grocery store's are in direct opposition. We want to get our shopping done quickly, before the kids get antsy, while the supermarket's agenda is to keep us in the store for as long as possible. These giant stores are designed to make us traipse from one end of the store to the other while tempting us to shop impulsively with each step.

THE BEST STRATEGY IS TO . . .
- Be realistic about shopping time.
- Avoid shopping at naptime.
- Eat before shopping.
- Come prepared.

Get to first base. You can have a more peaceful expedition by involving your kids. Ask them to pick out the broccoli and zucchini, to find the can of tomato sauce, or to help push the shopping cart. One mother I know approaches a shopping trip like a scavenger hunt; her kids love shopping and rarely fuss. But for those of us who have less time (and energy), I suggest simply making an effort to keep your child busy in an age-appropriate manner.

Leave early. Plan to arrive at the cashier before the whining, fidgeting, and crabbiness begin. Otherwise you're asking the kids to face the mouthwatering temptations at the checkout counter (the supermarket knows what it's doing) when they're running on empty. I know families who never buy their kids a treat, while others will buy treats from time to time. In my opinion, the question is not whether you buy a treat, it's whether your kids are able to hear the word "no" without having a meltdown. You don't need a principle about treats (save principles for bigger issues), but you do need skill at saying no and meaning it.

> ⇥ *Don't wait for problems before deciding to leave the store. Note how long it takes before your child gets antsy over the next few shopping expeditions, then plan to end your trips five or ten minutes earlier. You'll likely discover that your child is fairly consistent in her tolerance level; this is something you'll need to either respect or come prepared to deal with.*

Use the three R's. For all the problems that can't be averted, reframe, reflect, and resolve your way through them.

Control yourself, not your child. Here's a story from Sherri, mother of four-year-old Megan: "There were six people ahead of us in line. I was thinking if the line moved quickly enough, I'd make it home in just enough time for a business call I was expecting. Megan interrupted my thoughts: 'Can I have a chocolate bar?'

'No, it's almost lunchtime,' I replied. Megan zapped back with *'I hate you. You're the worst mommy.'* Then she threw herself on the ground and played dead. When I tried to lift her up, she went completely limp. I warned her of all sorts of punishments that were waiting for her if she didn't get up immediately (usually I'm more patient, but I didn't have time for antics). Once I *reflected* on the situation, I realized that my attempts to change Megan's behavior were not helping. If anything, they were aggravating things. So I opted out and went about my business, and without the motivation she was getting from me, Megan soon lost interest in her tantrum. Although I didn't get home in time for my call, I did get home with my self-respect intact."

WHAT'S REALISTIC?

According to an informal survey I did years ago, the average child puts up with shopping for:

- Five to ten minutes for toddlers.
- Ten to fifteen minutes for preschoolers.
- Twenty to thirty minutes for school-age kids.
- An indefinite time for teenagers, who outlast parents, hands down.

Take inventory. Like us, kids get cranky when they are tired, bored, or hungry. But the problem is that when a child misbehaves in public, parents tend to address the misbehavior and ignore the underlying problem. The best way to handle the situation is to respond to both ends of the equation. Let your child know that you don't condone his behavior, but at the same time, recognize and correct the fundamental problem.

Use stress prevention. A simple but essential strategy is to always carry snacks and other distractions in case shopping takes longer than anticipated. If you think ahead and take active steps, you'll have far fewer problems to deal with and will be better prepared should any occur. Stress prevention also includes assuming a less reactive mind-set. When parents are more relaxed, they have more fun with their kids, keep things in perspective, and are better able to handle the sore spots with love and humor.

If This Happens

Your youngster refuses to get into the car when it's time to go home.

She's Feeling

"I'm tired."

Don't Say

"If you get into the car now, I'll buy you an ice cream on the way home."

Instead, Say

Give your child motivation by saying, "When we get home, you can help me make a nice dinner."

•　　•　　•

If This Happens

You're almost at the cash register after waiting in line for fifteen minutes when your five-year-old yells, "Mommy, why is the fat lady taking so long?"

She's Feeling

"I'm curious."

Don't Say

"Shhh. That's not a nice way to talk."

Instead, Say

You apologize to the woman and, once you have a little privacy, ask your child, "Remember when your sister made fun of your freckles and you cried? Well, how do you think that woman feels about being called fat?"

• • •

If This Happens

Your kids, three, five, and six, are all whining at the same time. "Are we finished yet?" "Can I buy gum?" "It's my turn to push the cart."

They're Feeling

"We're bored."

Don't Say

"If you don't calm down, you'll all get a time-out as soon as we get home."

Instead, Say

You realize the kids are tired and that you pushed your luck by staying so long. You choose not to get upset, vow to wrap up the trip as quickly as possible, and ask playfully "Who wants to play I Spy?"

• • •

If This Happens

Your four-year-old refuses to take no for an answer. "Why can't I buy ice cream? You never let me buy anything good. Jordan gets to buy whatever he wants."

She's Feeling

"I feel jealous."

Don't Say

You react to everything your child says with, "Because I said so" or "That's not true. You got ice cream the last time we shopped" or "I don't care what Jordan gets."

Instead, Say

You know that extreme language is designed to make you feel guilty. You ask for clarification by saying, "I never let you buy anything?"

THINK IT THROUGH

Reframe

Take stock: "How can I change my shopping routine so it's less stressful?"

Reflect

Why are your shopping expeditions unpleasant?

_____

_____

_____

_____

Resolve

You can make the supermarket trek fun. All you need is a plan. Make a to-do list of the new way you plan to approach shopping trips.

_____

_____

_____

_____

SHYNESS
"Should I Be Worried?"

When my youngest daughter, Madison, was four years old, she'd hide behind me whenever unfamiliar guests came to our home. She'd sit through an entire dinner with her head turned away from anyone she didn't know well. I couldn't take her to children's programs because she wouldn't leave my side. At birthday parties, she would refuse to get off my lap. For the longest time, I worried that she had poor self-esteem. Today, however, Madison is an outgoing eight-year-old who plays soccer; in fact, she's the only girl on an all-boys team.

SHYNESS RED FLAGS
After the toddler years, if shyness interferes with a child's willingness or ability to participate in activities, like birthday parties and family gatherings, you should discuss the situation with your pediatrician. Shyness may be the result of anxiety, low self-esteem, or separation anxiety.

Young children are shy for two reasons: 1) a personality trait that will continue throughout the child's life, or 2) a common reaction to an unfamiliar situation. A shyness-prone youngster can be encouraged to feel more relaxed in social situations in the following ways.

Encourage, don't discourage. The number one question that parents ask me about a shy child is "Should I push her to socialize?" The answer is clearly *no*. The more you push your child, the greater she will resist. Instead, respect her shyness. Talk to her about her feelings. Let her know she's not alone. Give her examples from your own experience. Then help your child practice socializing at a pace that works for her. Be proactive by arriving at social events early so your child has a chance to adapt. Allow her to stay close by if that gives her a sense of comfort. Remember that shyness is one of her characteristics, not a weakness. On the other hand, don't be overprotective or overindulgent of a shyness-prone child. You may want to prevent her from feeling anxiety or distress. However, children overcome their problems by being challenged.

Promote alliances. A shy child may need help forming friendships. Encourage your child to invite friends over, and participate in activities with children of a similar age.

Connie, the mother of four-year-old Blake, told me this story. I want to share it with you because it demonstrates the importance of being open-minded. The summer camp Blake was attending offered a one-night sleepover toward the end of the session. Connie never mentioned it to Blake, because he was a painfully shy boy and she was certain he wouldn't want to go. But Blake learned about it from his counselor, who said, "You've got to come, it'll be awesome!" To her complete surprise, Blake asked to go. On the night of the sleepover, Connie fully expected a call instructing her to pick up Blake. But the only call she received was an enthusiastic one: "Good night, Mom. Good night, Dad, I gotta go, we're roasting marshmallows."

Become a good listener. Give your shy child plenty of opportunities to express her ideas in a nonthreatening environment. Mealtimes are an excellent time for this kind of sharing. Older siblings should be discouraged for speaking on behalf of a shy child.

Don't label your child. Avoid labeling, as this may serve as a self-fulfilling prophecy. Your child may hide behind the shyness and use it as an excuse not to socialize.

> ✺ *There's a difference between being an introvert and being shy. Some people are naturally more sociable than others. I, for one, am a homebody. I love to stay at home and work on my various ongoing projects. I've been like this my entire life. It's not that I don't enjoy company, it's just that I equally enjoy my own quiet activities. I am perfectly comfortable in social situations, but I would often rather stay at home than go out with friends. Some children are the same way. But in the end a child needs a balance between time spent alone and social activities.*

Be open. Discuss your child's shyness with her. The more you understand her feelings and concerns, the easier it will be to help her deal with them.

> ✺ *Don't use shame. Comments like "Stop acting like a baby" don't help even remotely.*

Differentiate between privacy and shyness. Respect your child's desire for privacy, which may appear as early as eighteen months.

As a final note to this chapter, and for shy children everywhere, let me repeat that shyness is a behavioral style, not a weakness. Your shy child is strong and capable, and by having confidence in her, you can help her achieve a higher comfort level in social situations.

THINK IT THROUGH

Reframe

Ask, "How am I helping my child to rise above her shyness?"

Reflect

Think of a recent situation where your little one's shyness was a problem. How did you handle your child's resistance or anxiety?

_____

_____

What did you learn from this episode?

_____

_____

If you could read your child's thoughts, what would she say about how you respond to her shyness?

_____

_____

Resolve

Map out a strategy to help your child feel more relaxed in social situations.

_____

_____

_____

_____

RED ALERT: Allow your child to develop social skills at his own pace, even if it makes you feel uneasy.

SKINNY KIDS
Busting the Myths

Eat, eat, eat—three words a skinny kid knows all too well. Many parents equate being skinny with being undernourished and feel compelled to push their kids to eat more. Yet encouraging a thin but healthy child to eat when she's no longer hungry may predispose her to an eating disorder or obesity down the road. For parents of otherwise healthy kids who happen to be lean, let's take a look at some of the hype that may be causing you grief.

- MYTH: *My child needs balanced meals.* It is unrealistic to expect a young child to eat all food groups at each meal. Instead, think in terms of a balanced week. As long as your child eats something from each food group during the course of the week, he'll meet his nutritional needs.
- MYTH: *My kids need vitamins.* Kids should get their nutrition from food. First, it's easy to satisfy a child's basic nutritional needs with food. Second, I feel strongly that a child shouldn't think she needs a pill to stay healthy. What's the silent message behind giving your child a daily pill? It tells kids that pills are good for them. And it says, "You lack wellness."
- MYTH: *My child needs to drink more milk because she doesn't eat well.* I know what you're going to say: "My daughter isn't a good eater. I give her extra milk so she'll get at least something nutritious." This kind of thinking gives rise to overdrinking and undereating habits. The easiest way to deal with this problem is to cut down on milk.

  HINT: This problem is particularly common in older toddlers and preschoolers who are still on a bottle. If your child is still hooked on a bottle after the age of two, I highly recommend that you wean her to a cup. She'll eat better once you do.

- MYTH: *He needs to eat more.* One of the most common misconceptions is how much food it takes for a young child to thrive. Parents more often than not believe a child needs more food than he actually does. That's one of the reasons why more than 20 percent of American kids are overweight. A young child will listen to her body and stop eating when she's no longer hungry. Trust your child, he knows more about what he needs to eat than you think.

- MYTH: *A lean child is more likely to get sick.* An underweight child is not more prone to infections, malnutrition, or vitamin deficiencies. He's just lean. Try to keep that in mind when you feel the urge to push your kids to eat more.

- MYTH: *Encouragement doesn't hurt.* While I've never seen a medical problem caused by being thin, I certainly have seen emotional and behavioral problems result from food battles. Ironically, the best way to encourage your child to eat more is to say nothing. The more relaxed everyone is at mealtime, the more likely your child will gradually improve her eating habits. Last year, Michael's mother came to my office because she thought her five-year-old was too thin. She was tired of fighting with him and wanted me to lay down the law. When I weighed and measured Michael and plotted his measurements, we discovered that Michael was gaining perfectly. He was taller than he was heavy, but his weight gain was more than adequate. His mother left the office determined not to say another word about his eating habits. A few months later, when she was back with another one of her children, I asked how things were going with Michael and his eating. She replied, "I need to take out a second mortgage to feed him." Obviously, in this situation, less was more.

Take "response-ability."

With some of the misconceptions cleared up, you should be able to deal with the pressure from other people or family members who complain that your child is too skinny. Skinny is good. What's not good? The power struggles and stress that inevitably develop when adults pressure kids to eat. Although restraint takes a great deal of self-control, you'll do yourself and your child an enormous favor by not making an issue of her eating habits. Give her healthy choices, then trust her to make the right ones.

THINK IT THROUGH

Reframe

Ask, "Am I putting unnecessary pressure on my child to eat?"

Reflect

Task: Record a mealtime using a video camera or tape player. Play it back, and keep an eye on you. What do you see?

_____

_____

What did you learn?

_____

_____

TIP: Notice the positive and negative ways you negotiate with your kids around food.

Resolve

You are the architect of the family unit. Create a solid foundation by using mealtime as an opportunity to strengthen bonds between family members.

I plan to

_____

_____

_____

SLEEP ISSUES (FOR BABIES)

The Down-to-Earth Guide to Getting More Sleep

If you are desperate for more sleep, and you've already tried everything but nothing has worked, then you're probably making the same mistakes many other loving and caring parents make when they're exhausted and frustrated. Your baby isn't a poor sleeper; actually, you've been inadvertently encouraging her to wake up every few hours. Most likely you've already been bombarded by advice from friends, your mother or your mother-in-law, and your pediatrician. You've been told to give your baby some cereal before you put her to bed, let her cry it out, keep a night-light on in the bedroom, bring her into bed, or be patient because it's "just a phase." This kind of advice usually doesn't help, and it may even make things worse.

Waking up in the night is perfectly natural. In fact, we all wake up when we're in a shallow sleep, but we comfort ourselves back to sleep by following a soothing routine. For instance, I curl up in my favorite position, readjust my pillow, and then nod off. But if you have unwittingly trained your child to fall asleep by depending on you, she will need you whenever she reaches a shallow sleep state. By rocking, feeding, singing, walking, or jiggling your baby to sleep, you are guaranteeing that she will wake from a shallow sleep because she needs whatever it is she's grown accustomed to in order to doze off again. In essence, you are teaching her to wake up.

> *Did you know that the average adult needs a minimum of seven and half hours of sleep each night?*

I want to clarify one thing: There is nothing wrong with rocking your baby to sleep or getting up at night to soothe or comfort her, if that's what you want to do. But let's say that, for whatever reason, you don't want to get up at night anymore; then it goes without saying that you need to make some changes.

Currently there are two approaches to a baby's sleep habits. There are parents and experts who believe that babies need to learn to fall asleep independently using variations of the cry-it-out method. Then there are those in favor of shared sleeping, also known as co-sleeping, and the family bed, whose supporters believe that a baby needs his parents right next to him in order to feel a sense of security.

For the parents who are desperate for more sleep but don't want to let their baby cry it out any more than they want to get into the family-bed routine, I've developed a simple strategy.

> *There is enormous pressure on mothers to ignore their own needs. We're made to feel guilty, selfish, and uncaring for wanting uninterrupted sleep. But a mother's needs are not trivial or secondary. Your baby will benefit from your sense of well-being, and she'll respect you because of the respect you show for yourself.*

> *Did you know that sleep deprivation is associated with accelerated aging, high blood pressure, and diabetes?*

Becoming a Sleep Mentor

Jan and Steve. This charming couple, unaware that bad habits were being established, rocked Hal for forty minutes each night before he nodded off. This wasn't a problem at first, but by nine months of age, Hal was too heavy for his mom to carry. Hal knew no other way to go to sleep, and what followed was months of frustration.

Helen and Rick. Helen wasn't worried about letting nine-month-old Manny cry for a few moments, but Rick couldn't bear listening to his little one in distress. At the first sign, Rick would dash into Manny's room and pick her up. The amazing thing was, one winter when Helen and the baby were visiting her parents down south, Grandma suggested that Helen allow little Manny to fuss for a moment before intervening to see whether she would fall back to sleep on her own. Much to Helen's surprise, the first night and every one thereafter, Manny grunted and squirmed briefly before dropping right back to sleep. Which meant that all along, Rick had been waking Manny up, not the other way around.

Tanya. Being a single mother meant that there was no one to take turns with during the night. So, Tanya and little Susie shared her bed from the start. But Tanya was worried that she'd roll over, and as a result she slept only fitfully. After six months, Tanya was drained. She wasn't meeting deadlines at work, and she was short-tempered at home. Tanya felt "stuck"; she didn't want to share her bed with Susie any longer, but she couldn't stand to let her cry.

Many parents assume that a child's poor sleep habits are a stage that will eventually disappear. But in reality, old patterns of behavior will not fade away until parents take active steps to encourage new ones. Recent research shows that preschoolers with sleep problems are more likely to have behavioral and learning problems, so I highly recommend that you deal with these problems early on.

As a working mom with young children, I have to be practical when it comes to my little ones' sleep habits, as I suspect you do, too. I want to give my kids all the love and attention they need; nonetheless, I absolutely need uninterrupted sleep. What I have come to see is that these priorities are not mutually exclusive. The following guidelines will help you get your baby's sleep on track in a manner that respects her need for comfort and meets your need for more sleep.

The younger the baby, the easier it is to teach her how to fall asleep independently. I suggest that you begin to work on sleep habits once your baby is gaining nicely and well established in her feeding routine. Generally speaking, you should begin by two months of age.

Sooner, not later. It is easier to put a baby or child to bed before he's totally exhausted, because it's easier for him to deal with the stress of separation while he still has some reserve. If you start the bedtime routine at the first sign of tiredness, he'll doze off with less fussing.

Day/night reversal. Many babies sleep for long periods during the day and are completely awake at bedtime. But recent research suggests that babies can learn the difference between day and night early on if they're given the proper signals. You can do this by exaggerating the difference: In the daytime, talk to your baby while you feed her, stroke her, play energetic music, keep her bedroom bright and colorful, and change activities as often as needed. At nighttime, darken the room, whisper, don't stroke her during feedings, skip diaper changes if at all possible, then gently pop her back into bed.

Create rituals. Babies thrive on routine. Anything a parent can do to make the child's world more predictable will help him gain a sense of control over events in his life. Try different routines until you find one that allows your baby to wind down. This may mean a massage, a bath, story time, or feeding. *TIP:* Don't let your baby fall asleep during the bedtime ritual.

Eyes wide open. After feeding and the bedtime ritual, it's time to put your sleepy but awake baby into bed. If she cries, and most likely she will, pat her on the back and whisper words of reassurance: "Shhh—it's okay. Mommy's here." Comfort her when she cries, but *stop patting her when she's quiet,* otherwise you'll simply be exchanging one bad habit for another. On average, a baby takes five to twenty minutes to fall asleep. Guide and support her through this learning period, and she'll soon be nodding off on her own. If she cries for a prolonged period, pat her gently, jiggle her, sing to her, even give her a top-up of milk, but don't let her fall asleep in your arms.

Truthfully, the biggest challenge is the one that takes place in our heads. Many parents struggle with the question "Am I hurting my baby by encouraging her to be independent?" Let me reassure you, independence is a good thing. Not only because it gives you more free time and because you'll get more sleep (although who's complaining?), but because it boosts self-esteem. The true first step to solving sleep problems is to wholeheartedly believe in your baby. Most babies are born strong (just go take a look at your own baby pictures and you'll see what I mean). Work with the assumption that your baby's capable and tough, and you'll send the message that you have confidence in her.

What to expect. It will take determination, resolve, and stamina not to cave in when your infant cries, especially the first few nights. Your baby will cry, and despite your reassurance, patting, and high hopes, things may very well get worse before they get better. Your baby may cry harder and longer as she tries to convince you to revert to the old routine. But although you may find it hard to do, if you persist a little longer, your baby will discover new ways of comforting herself back to sleep. How long it takes will depend on your child's age and temperament. Many parents expect the worst and are pleasantly surprised by how quickly the baby learns a new routine.

Talk shop. In my office, I consider it a matter of respect to explain to a baby or child what I'm going to do before doing it. For instance, I jabber away while I'm examining a newborn: "Now I'm going to check your hips, and then I'm going to shine a light in your eyes." I carry on a conversation as if the baby understands me; I know she doesn't understand my words, but my tone of voice hopefully conveys reassurance. Talk your baby through sleep problems in the same way by saying, "Okay, pumpkin, it's bedtime. I know you like to fall asleep with a bottle, but you're tough, and I know you can learn to fall asleep without one." If your baby cries, reassure her by saying, "It's okay, you're a strong baby and I have confidence in you."

Pacifier penalties. In my experience, a pacifier causes as many problems as it solves. A baby who is put to sleep with a pacifier will wake up from a shallow sleep state when his prop is lost. He can't doze off without it, yet he can't find it on his own. You're better off to put your baby to bed without a pacifier and avoid this trap altogether.

Weed out nighttime feedings. Many parents assume that a baby wakes up at night because he's hungry. According to the American Academy of Pediatrics, by the time your baby is four months of age, he should be able to go eight hours without feeding. But what if your baby disagrees with the American Academy of Pediatrics and continues to want to feed in the night? Ask your pediatrician whether your baby is gaining well enough to skip a nighttime feeding. In reality, most babies wake up because they've reached a shallow level of sleep and don't know how to get back to sleep without you. *They nurse to go back to sleep, not to satisfy hunger.* To help your baby learn how to fall back asleep soundly when he's in a shallow sleep, give him an opportunity to comfort himself when he begins to squirm. Don't rush in. If it doesn't look like he's able to get back to sleep, then go and comfort him. But remember to put him back in the crib while he's awake so he gains the experience of falling asleep independently.

> ◄ *One strategy that has helped many babies under my care to sleep longer is to give the little one an extra feeding before you go to bed. You should be able to quietly feed the baby without actually waking him up.*

Older babies. Last year I did an informal survey and found that 70 percent of the parents who tried to redirect an infant's sleep habits before the age of ten months were successful. After this age, things got trickier. Can we honestly expect an older baby, who has fallen asleep against her father's chest since day one, to change without some degree of emotional upheaval or resistance? Aren't we setting ourselves up for frustration and failure if we trick ourselves into believing we can do it painlessly? For an easygoing baby, a little angel, it may not be too challenging. But for the vast majority of babies, it will be more difficult. If you're wondering, "Can't we just do the same thing we did with the younger baby?," theoretically, you can. But practically speaking, some babies find it more stressful to have you in the room. For easygoing babies, the guidelines I discussed earlier will work, and you won't need to feel conflicted. But an older or more intense baby will resist the change. Let's look at some of the strategies that will ease the transition and minimize crying and stress.

Warm up. Perhaps the most difficult aspect about changing sleeptime habits is that we're trying to suck and blow at the same time. In other words, we are quick to respond to the baby's needs during waking hours, but come bedtime, we turn off our responsiveness and encourage independence. This makes for a confusing discrepancy between our daytime and nighttime habits. If you minimize the gap between your day- and nighttime routines, you minimize difficulties. I suggest moms and dads work on daytime independence before working on nighttime issues. Many parents have difficulty with this concept because they equate independence with negligence. However, what's missing is a middle-ground approach where parents respond to a baby's needs but in a way that provides her the opportunity to exercise her independence.

Practice the rule of fives. As you direct an older baby to fall asleep independently, give her five-minute practice intervals. Put her in the crib after the bedtime routine; if she's still crying after five minutes, take her out of the crib and settle her in your arms. Five minutes in and five minutes out, and so on. Keep doing this in-and-out routine until your baby falls asleep. You can stretch or reduce the period of time before going into the baby's room as needed. The older or more intense the baby, the longer it will take. But I suspect this transition is harder on you than it is on your child.

>> *Think of the direction of your child's sleep habits as an ongoing process. There will be times when you need to go back to square one and retrain your child anew, such as after an illness, teething, or a vacation.*

The bottom line. Whether or not your baby sleeps through the night has nothing to do with your parenting skills. If redirecting your baby's sleep habits is causing you stress, then take a break and try again later.

>> *I can't very well discuss sleep habits without mentioning the importance of placing healthy babies on their back to sleep in order to reduce the risk of crib death.*

Myth

"I'll get more sleep if I give my baby a pacifier."

Fact

Until your baby has the coordination to put the pacifier back in her mouth—which generally develops by three to six months of age—you'll be up plenty of times each night popping it back in for her.

• • •

The Myth

"The only way I can get my baby to sleep is by nursing her or giving her a bottle."

Fact

Your baby can unlearn this habit, but it won't happen without your direction. Beware: Going to bed with a bottle can lead to severe dental decay and ear infections.

·　　·　　·

Myth

"My baby will be emotionally scarred if I let her cry."

Fact

There's a difference between restless noises and crying. Take a moment before rushing in to determine whether your child is fitful or fretful. A fretful baby may need you, but a fitful one needs sleep.

·　　·　　·

Myth

"The best place for a baby is in bed with you."

Fact

In a study published in the September 2000 issue of *Pediatrics Electronic Pages* (the Internet extension of *Pediatrics*, the scientific journal of the American Academy of Pediatrics), researchers warned parents about the danger of bed sharing due to the risk of suffocation. In the fall of 1999, the U.S. Consumer Product Safety Commission warned parents about the dangers of cosleeping based on sixty-four infant deaths due to suffocation. On a personal note, I know of a nanny who fell asleep and rolled over and suffocated the child in her care.

·　　·　　·

Myth

"I'll wake the rest of the family up if I let the baby cry."

Fact

The baby may fuss for only a moment before dropping off to sleep. Plus, you don't know whether or not the older kids will sleep through the fuss unless you try.

•   •   •

Myth

"The baby is waking up because of gas."

Fact

The problem with this observation is that an angry baby looks much the same as a gassy one, except one passes gas and the other doesn't. They both get red in the face and pull up their legs. The gassy baby may need burping or a change in formula. The angry baby needs to be comforted, but once he's settled, he needs the opportunity to comfort himself to sleep.

I can't think of anything that's more stressful than dealing with sleeptime issues, except perhaps dealing with everyone's opinions about what we're doing wrong and what we need to do to get it right. It's hard enough to deal with our own emotions without having to defend ourselves against others. One way of handling friends or family members who feel they need to express their opinions is to say something like "Thanks for your suggestions, but let's agree to disagree on this one."

Take "response-ability."

Use the three R's to gain a better understanding of the feedback loop between you and your baby. If you do, you'll be rewarded with a good night's sleep and a well-rested and more contented baby.

> ⊰ *The best predictor of sleep problems in preschool and school-age children is a history of sleep problems under the age of two. In other words, the sleep habits you establish now may persist well beyond infancy and subsequently affect a child's behavior. If that's not motivation to work on sleep issues, I don't know what is.*

THINK IT THROUGH

Reframe

Contemplate: "How am I influencing my baby's sleep patterns?"

Reflect

When you choose a way of putting your baby to sleep, you choose the consequences that go with it. Define this relationship.

The habit

The consequence

_____

The habit

_____

The consequence

_____

The way I put my baby to bed is

_____

I put my baby to bed this way because

_____

I think

_____

I feel

_____

Resolve

Think in great detail about what it is you are going to do differently. I plan to

_____

I am choosing this because

_____

The hardest part will be

_____

I plan to deal with this by

_____

I want

_____

I believe

_____

I know

_____

RED ALERT: If I could wrap up the debate on the best way to put your baby to sleep, I would. But there is no one right answer. The best advice I can give you is this: Become informed, examine the issues, and follow your gut instincts.

SLEEP ISSUES (FOR OLDER KIDS)
The Down-to-Earth Guide to Getting More Sleep

All of a sudden, everyone seems to be talking about the importance of getting enough sleep. Its status has changed from luxury to necessity. Current studies prove that sleep deprivation has a powerful negative impact on the body, mind, heart, and soul. It leads to depression, irritability, forgetfulness, poor concentration, anxiety, lethargy, car accidents, and vulnerability to infections. A sleep-deprived youngster may experience learning problems and behavioral difficulties such as hyperactivity, crankiness, whining, and temper tantrums.

> *An exhausted parent equals a tired child.*

The biggest challenge is trying to find a balance between a child's need for comfort and a parent's need for sleep. As mentioned in the previous chapter, there are two opposing schools of thought on putting a youngster to bed and encouraging him to stay there. But I know many parents, myself included, for whom neither of these approaches has worked. As a result, I have been helping parents resolve sleep problems using an approach that is based on mutual respect: for your child and for yourself.

Good-Night Primer

Create rituals. A child loves rituals and routines; they teach him what to expect and make a complex world more predictable. Bedtime routines help children gear down and prepare for the night. To begin with, keep after-dinner activities mellow, and allow approximately twenty minutes for a bath, getting on pajamas, brushing teeth, and a story, and repeat the same bedtime preparations each night without variation. If you're consistent with bedtime, your child's inner clock will adjust to the routine. You can take this a step further if needed and make a bedtime poster that illustrates step by step what your child must do to get ready for bed. The poster becomes the boss, eliminating a tug-of-war between parent and child.

"Bedtime!?" Maggie's four-year-old stepdaughter, April, often cries during her weekend visits. April refuses to stay in bed and complains that she wants to go home. Out of pure desperation, Maggie sometimes lets her conk out on the couch. The problem is that when Maggie carries April to bed, the child often awakes and then stays up past midnight. As a general rule of thumb, the best time to put a child to bed is when she's tired but not overtired. Because bedtime involves parting from intimate relationships and letting go of fun and excitement, children are better able to deal with these demands when they have their wits about them. Early signs of tiredness include yawning, thumb sucking or other self-comforting habits, loss of coordination, whining, giddiness, and slowing down. Arguing, tantrums, rowdiness, crying easily, and aggressive play are behaviors that suggest you missed the target, and the best thing to do now is get your child to bed as quickly as possible.

> ↝ *Napping late in the day may interfere with bedtime. Try putting your child down for an earlier nap if getting her to bed at a reasonable hour is an issue.*

Begin at the end. If you're in the habit of lying down with your child until he falls asleep, think about whether you'll still want to do this in the months or even years to come. Recognize that it's easier to avoid establishing a bad habit than it is to try and break it later.

Encourage transitional objects. "Blankies" and bears can provide enormous comfort to a young child and make the transition from being together to being alone a soft and gentle one.

Never go to bed angry. That was my Buby's motto. Although her intent was to encourage us children to resolve our differences, this same philosophy serves as a guide for how I currently manage nighttime sleep issues. I had one family who was having so much difficulty keeping three-year-old Tim in bed that, on the advice of their pediatrician, they held his bedroom door shut and refused to open it unless Tim was in bed. To be sure, Tim's parents felt miserable; they didn't like using strong-arm tactics, but they didn't know what else to do.

At times we have to move backward before progress is possible. I realized that Tim had negative associations with his bedroom that were complicating his willingness to go to bed. For starters, I asked the parents to spend time playing with Tim in his bedroom, and to stop sending him there for time-out. Gradually, Tim stopped thinking of his bedroom as hostile territory, and we were able to move forward. Here's how:

Bedtime discipline. Let's remember our earlier commitment to meeting our children's nighttime needs, and think about how we can respectfully do so without neglecting our own needs. Start off by using the "one callback" rule, which is a way to give your child a final request before you leave her room. Ask, "Is there anything you want before I go downstairs? Do you need to go to the bathroom? Do you want a glass of water? How about one more kiss?" Most kids, given the opportunity, will ask for something. Finally, to help your older child make the transition from the security of your company to the bigger world, ask him to pick a favorite place to think about in his mind, and reassure him that thinking about it will help him fall asleep.

"What if he keeps getting out of bed?" How you respond to antics after you've left the room will determine whether they continue or not. I suggested to Tim's parents that if he got out of bed, they should calmly but firmly take him by the hand, redirect him back to bed, and simply say, *"It's bedtime."* No hugs, snuggles, or kisses. The first night Tim snuck out of bed ten times before he fell asleep. His parents did as I suggested. The next night, he got up fifteen times, and the fourth night twenty times. I had prepared Mom and Dad for the likelihood that Tim would get worse before he got better. In effect, his behavior was saying, "Aren't you guys going to yell at me to get back into bed?" By the fifth night, Tim surprised everyone by playing quietly in his room before falling asleep. Go figure!

Sleeptime Shenanigans

Here is a glance at some of the problems I'm asked to help parents deal with daily. Learning to respond to our children instead of react to them is an essential lesson, and one that enables parents to act in a dignified manner.

The Sore Spot

"My child won't stay in bed."

The Likely Cause

You are likely reacting to his sneaking out of bed in a manner that is encouraging it.

The Solution

When your child gets out of bed, say in a neutral but firm voice, "Back to bed," without giving her negative or positive attention.

. . .

The Sore Spot

"My child wakes up in the night and then refuses to go back to sleep."

The Likely Cause

There are secondary gains that are making it worthwhile for your child to stay up.

The Solution

The middle of the night is not the time for snuggles, hugs, or kisses. Handle the nighttime wake-ups in a matter-of-fact but respectful manner.

. . .

The Sore Spot

"My child won't fall asleep unless I lie down with her."

The Likely Cause

Your child has learned to fall asleep with you by her side; without you, she doesn't feel right.

The Solution

Let your child know you have confidence in her ability to master her emotions by giving her the room to do so. Your child is not going to give up this habit without a nudge from you.

•   •   •

The Sore Spot

"My children ignore me when I call bedtime."

The Likely Cause

Is naptime too late in the day? Are you missing tiredness cues? Alternatively, you may be giving your kids the impression that it's okay to ignore you.

The Solution

Make naptime earlier. Watch for the earliest signs of fatigue. And use the A, B, C, and D's of good listening (see "Listening," page 150).

•   •   •

The Sore Spot

"My four-year-old refuses to sleep through the night."

The Likely Cause

Think about what happens when she wakes up and what she needs to get back to sleep, and realize this is the problem. For instance, if you need to lie down with your child to help her fall back to sleep, then this is the habit that needs to change. *RED ALERT:* Be careful not to exchange one bad habit for another.

The Solution

Retrain your child to sleep through the night by helping her learn the self-comforting skills she needs to nod off. If your child wakes up in the night, calmly walk her back to her room, say, "Bedtime," and skip the hugs. You may need to do this many times the first few nights, but by the third night or so, she'll catch on.

· · ·

The Sore Spot

"My toddler won't go to bed without a bottle."

The Likely Cause

Your child has been conditioned to fall asleep by taking a bottle. Beware; this habit may lead to serious dental caries and ear infections.

The Solution

It's important that you stop this habit for medical reasons. Your child needs to learn to fall asleep without props.

· · ·

The Sore Spot

"My child complains of being afraid."

The Likely Cause

You may be reinforcing your child's fears through your response to them. If your child's fears interfere with his daily activities, or are escalating over time, speak with your pediatrician about the problem.

The Solution

If simple reassurance isn't enough, tell your child you'll check on him in five minutes. He'll feel less alone if he knows you're coming back. And more often than not, he will be asleep by the time you return.

⇥ Many parents confuse placating with nurturing. Placating involves giving the child what he wants so he won't be angry or upset, while nurturing means meeting his needs. There are far fewer sleep problems when parents put their energy into nurturing instead of placating.

Take "response-ability."

Ultimately, the best piece of advice I can give you is to make getting a good night's rest a priority in your life. Your family as a whole will reap the benefits. But no matter what, at least remember my grandmother's motto: "Don't go to bed angry." Committing to this policy encourages you to recognize the innocence of your child's behavior, and it reminds you of the need for self-control and perspective.

THINK IT THROUGH

Reframe

Think about: "How am I feeding in to my child's sleep problems?"

Reflect

Empower yourself by acknowledging what you are doing that's not working, and do something different.

Use the acronym S-T-O-P to clarify your end of the equation.

See. Replay in your mind the situation that is causing you grief._____

_____

Think. How does your thinking influence the situation?

_____

_____

Observe. Take a step backward and notice your body language, tone of voice, and facial expressions.

_____

Put it together. How do your mental and emotional contributions influence your knee-jerk reactions?

_____

_____

Resolve

Let's use the feedback loop to change ineffective patterns of behavior.

My four-year-old wakes up each night and refuses to go back to sleep.

My reaction is: I get in bed with her.

The cause-and-effect relationship is: My child wakes me up because she knows that I will get in bed with her.

By changing my end of the equation, I can inspire a different reaction from my child.

In the future, I plan to _____

_____

_____

The problem: _____

_____

My reaction is: _____

_____

The cause-and-effect relationship is: _____

_____

In the future, I plan to _____

_____

HINT: Children benefit from firm, consistent, and clear guidelines. When your child is getting up for the tenth time, he needs you to draw the line. Being firm is not a sign of neglect. Rather, it means you are willing to do what's best for your child, even if you find it hard to do.

SPOILING AND UNSPOILING
Encouraging an Attitude of Gratitude

SELF-QUIZ
- Does your child bully you into buying him things?
- Does your child argue with you when he doesn't get his way?
- Do you buy your kids things to avoid a scene?
- Do your kids ask *you* to fetch things for them?
- Do you feel like a servant?
- Is it easier to do something yourself rather than ask your child to do it?

If you answered yes to any of these questions, then you need to read this chapter.

For many parents, saying the word "no" is enormously complicated, even impossible. As a result, some children get whatever they want, whenever they want it. But the truly sad thing about permissive parenting is that children ultimately pay the price. A spoiled child will probably have difficulty with peers, and most likely with adult relationships, too; and sadly enough, he may never value the good things in his life, because to him the cup is always half empty.

MYTHS ABOUT SPOILING
You will not spoil your child if you:
- Pick up a baby when he cries.
- Carry a toddler when he asks.
- Buy a toy for a child.

PARENTS MAY HAVE DIFFICULTY SAYING NO BECAUSE . . .

- They feel guilty about upsetting the child.
- They want to be liked.
- They want to avoid a tantrum or whining.
- They are afraid of depriving the child.
- They feel uncertain of their ability to make the right decision.
- They want to raise their kids differently than their parents raised them.

Here are some guidelines to help you learn to say no, which is an essential aspect of raising unspoiled children.

Mean what you say. Learn to say no without waffling. If you say no and change your mind five minutes later, you've taught your child that it pays to pester or be persistent.

Don't end with: "Okay?" You don't need to feel apologetic for saying no to your child, and you don't need your child's permission. Ending a sentence with "Okay?" tells your child that the subject is open for discussion, in which case you'd better be prepared for arguments.

Be empathetic. You can acknowledge your child's feelings without giving in to them by saying, "I know you're angry that you can't stay up late, but it's bedtime."

Use a heightened awareness. If you have any doubts about how to respond to your child, ask yourself, "What am I teaching her by giving in?"

Don't bargain. Avoid falling into the trap of needing to promise something in exchange for cooperation. Bargaining teaches your child to wheel and deal, and eventually it will cost more to get less.

You don't need lengthy explanations. It's not a bad policy to give your child an explanation when you say no, but keep it short, simple, and age-appropriate. If your child has a tendency to argue, don't defend your decision; just let him know the topic isn't open for debate.

> *Buying a toy doesn't spoil a child, but buying a toy because your child won't take no for an answer does.*

Don't undermine each other. Parents need to support each other's decisions whether they agree or not, otherwise children learn to play one parent against the other. If you disagree with your partner, discuss it privately and work out a strategy to deal with your differences. This is particularly important in blended or separated families, where every decision is fraught with possible complications and underlying meaning.

Unspoiling

Parents want their kids to be happy and appreciative, but many of us unwittingly foster dissatisfaction and negativity by encouraging attitudes of entitlement: "It's my right to get whatever I want." The way to teach your child an attitude of gratitude is not through giving more attention, more time, or more goods; it's through fostering a sense of appreciation by setting more limits and having higher expectations.

Look for the good. You can teach your children gratitude by taking the time to focus on the good things that happen each day. If we teach our kids to notice the good, they feel happier and have a more positive view of the world. I make it a habit to ask my kids every night at the dinner table, "Tell me about the best thing that happened today." Now I no longer need to ask, they just tell me.

More than manners. By teaching a child to say thank you, you're doing more than instilling good manners. You're teaching him to acknowledge the things that others do on his behalf, to become less self-centered, and to have respect and empathy for others.

Raise your expectations. Chores teach children to contribute to the family and to give of themselves. Your child will live up (or down) to whatever expectations you have of her. If you teach your child to clean up after herself, she will do so. On the other hand, if your child learns that she can leave a mess and you'll take care of it, then that is what will happen. Kids must learn to pitch in to help the family run smoothly; children as young as three can be given official chores. The same thing goes for service calls. A common scenario is this: A child is watching television and calls out, "Mom, can I have a glass of water?" Before you jump up and get it, ask yourself, "What am I teaching my child?" Some parents feel uncomfortable encouraging a child to be independent. They feel they're being neglectful or uncaring. But a child will benefit more from learning to be self-reliant than from being served.

Live by example. Our children learn the biggest lessons from how we live, moment to moment. If you complain about all the injustices you face on a day-to-day basis, you teach your children to focus on problems and to view themselves as victims of circumstances. But if you are able to rise above the problems, and remain appreciative and even optimistic, you're more likely to enjoy each and every day and help your children do the same.

Take "response-ability."

Although it is often easier to cave in to our kids' demands, we are not doing them a favor in the long run. When you realize the importance of setting clear limits, you are better able to hold your ground and do so in a calm and respectful manner. Know that you are helping your child to become a fine, appreciative person.

THINK IT THROUGH

Reframe

Begin by asking yourself, "How do I spoil my child?"

Reflect

Use the acronym S-T-O-P to clarify your end of the equation.

See. Replay in your mind the situation that is causing you grief.

Think. How does my thinking influence the situation?

Observe. Take a step backward and notice your body language, tone of voice, and facial expressions.

Put it together. How do your mental and emotional contributions influence your knee-jerk reactions? What adjustments do you need to make to help you respond more constructively?

Resolve

Use the following vignettes to devise new approaches to old problems.

Your four-year-old wants an ice-cream cone and won't take no for an answer.

Your knee-jerk reaction is

_____

But you stop yourself and instead you

_____

Your five-year-old is crying because she asked for a vanilla milkshake, and now she's changed her mind and wants a chocolate one.

Your knee-jerk reaction is

_____

But you stop yourself and instead you

_____

You agreed to take your son bowling, but he's complaining because you won't allow him to bring a friend along.

Your knee-jerk reaction is

_____

But you stop yourself and instead you

_____

SPORTS AND PARENTS
Enjoying Without Destroying

D id you know that 75 percent of kids give up their favorite sport by age thirteen? According to Michael Pfahl, executive director of the National Youth Sport Coaches Association, the number one reason kids quit is that they stop having fun. Painful as it is to admit, parents have a great deal to do with this. In the year 2000, the National Association of Sports Officials recorded more than a hundred assaults on umpires and referees. Now, I'm no sports expert, but I know what I'm talking about when it comes to parenting. And I know for a fact that parents need to monitor their own behavior and show more restraint in the bleachers. A tragic example occurred in July 2000 when Michael Costin, who was coaching a hockey practice, was beaten to death by a disgruntled parent. This brutal example of sideline rage prompted a growing awareness of the need to teach appropriate bleacher behavior. No more hollering from the sidelines, fighting with the coach, whining, or finger-pointing.

This chapter is not about teaching our kids to be better sports or to try harder on the field. It's about parents learning to play fair and knowing how to support the emotional and physical wellness of the child, win or lose. It's about learning to control your anger before it controls you.

Stop yelling. Ask any kid how she feels about her parents yelling from the sidelines and you'll get the same answer: "I hate it." Coaches feel the same way. This is the single biggest turnoff to kids. It embarrasses and angers them. In the words of one twelve-year-old soccer player: "What do my parents expect? I'm already playing as hard as I can." Yelling negative comments, insults, or criticism from the sidelines only hurts, it does nothing to inspire. Comments from the bleachers should be positive or not made at all.

Be a good sport. Part of playing sports is learning to cope with frustration and disappointment. You can help by setting a good example. For instance, if the other team plays a great game, there's nothing wrong with congratulating them and doing so without making excuses or blaming the goalie for the performance of your child's team. Praise all the players, not just the ones you were rooting for.

Learn to calm down. If you find yourself getting worked up or overheated at a game, take a breather. But whatever you do, never ever yell at your child, another parent, the coach, or the referee. Nothing justifies this kind of behavior.

Motivate rather than irritate. There's a fine line between motivating your child and pushing too hard. Your child's response is the best gauge on whether you're overdoing it. If your child does not share your enthusiasm for the sport, then rethink his involvement. I don't believe in pressuring a child to play, whether you've paid for new equipment or not.

Coach rather than criticize. Your kids don't need a running commentary about their mistakes. Many of us have a tendency to focus on our children's flaws and forget to praise them for their accomplishments. I'm the first to admit that I've made this mistake. My son is a terrific soccer player, but for some reason he has a tendency to space out after halftime. Years ago I would nag Max (way too many times) to keep his mind on the game. One day it struck me that I was going about things the wrong way. Max needed motivation, not criticism. Now I limit my comments to positive ones, and while Max may not be the next Pele, he is playing harder and having more fun.

Don't focus on winning. Whatever happened to the attitude "it's not whether you win or lose, it's how you play the game"? We'd be helping our kids a great deal by returning to this belief system.

Teach by example. We teach our kids many positive and negative lessons without even saying a word. My eight-year-old daughter plays on a boys' soccer team (we didn't realize when she tried out it was a boys' team). But she made the team and decided to stick with it. It hasn't been easy (I'll spare you the details). At her last practice, I watched in amazement as the fathers who were assisting systematically ignored her. Even when she was in front of a wide-open net, they'd kick the ball to a boy instead. Like father, like son? It's up to you to determine the kind of example you want to set, and hopefully you'll choose to make it a good one.

> ⇥ *Watch what you say from the sidelines. Here are a couple of the comments made by parents I heard last week at my son's soccer game: "Stop playing like a girl" and "I didn't come to watch you do nothing. Move your butt!" Such remarks are disrespectful and unhelpful.*

Stop pushing. Sometimes the line between who's on the team and who's on the sidelines can get a little fuzzy. When parents live vicariously through their kids, winning or losing takes precedence over whether or not the child tried hard or had fun. Do you give your child the cold shoulder because he flubbed? If so, check your motives and expectations before you gear up for the next game. If the majority of kids drop out of sports by age thirteen, wouldn't a more balanced approach be one where winning is secondary to fitness and fun? In this scenario, mistakes would be met with encouragement, and youngsters would get unconditional approval for participating, doing their best, and having fun. In the big picture, wouldn't these kinds of attitudes be a bigger accomplishment?

⇥ I've known kids to come to my office faking an injury so I would provide them with an "out" from parents who would not take no for an answer.

Take "response-ability."
Okay, moms and dads, it's time we blow the whistle on our own behavior and stop confusing having fun with needing to win.

THINK IT THROUGH

Reframe

Use the three R's to monitor your own behavior and understand how you rank. To assist you past first base, ask yourself, "How do I behave in the bleachers?"

Reflect

Think of the positive and negative ways you interact before, after, and during games. What would the parent sitting next to you say about how you behave?

_____

_____

Resolve

What is your game plan? Map out a strategy so everyone comes out a winner.

_____

_____

STUTTERING
Promote Free Speech

> *One out of twenty children stutters between the ages of two and five years. Seventy-five percent of these children will stop stuttering without receiving any help.*

"What Should I Do?"

Should every child who stutters be referred to a speech pathologist? Five percent of all kids stutter at some point during their childhood, and the vast majority will stop stuttering without any intervention. How do you know whether a child needs to see a speech pathologist? Pediatricians don't spend a great deal of time studying language or speech difficulties in medical school or during their residency training, which is one reason why you'll find a huge discrepancy in referral patterns. I refer: 1) any child who is anxious about speaking; 2) when there is a family history of stuttering; 3) stuttering that persists after the preschool period; 4) if a child stutters for more than a few months. In the meantime, you can do a great deal to help a child who stutters. The following is a primer on the attitudes and strategies that are most beneficial.

MYTH: EMOTIONAL PROBLEMS CAUSE STUTTERING
Recent studies show no difference between emotional problems in children who stutter compared to those who don't.

Speak slowly. By modeling slow and relaxed speech, you will help your child to do the same. Apparently, we should all try to speak more like Mr. Rogers!

Pause before responding. You can change the pace of your child's speech by waiting a few moments before responding to him.

Stop interrupting. Allow your child to talk without interruptions, which will enable her to express herself freely.

FAMOUS PEOPLE WHO STUTTERED
- Marilyn Monroe
- Winston Churchill
- Carly Simon
- John Updike

Set aside time. In today's fast-paced lifestyle, little time is devoted to chatting. A child who stutters will become more confident if given opportunities to speak in a relaxed atmosphere.

Don't make her compete. In some families, kids compete with one another just to get a word in edgewise.

Don't speak for your kids. If your child stutters, wait quietly until he finishes his thoughts. Don't speak for him.

Make eye contact. By maintaining eye contact with your child, you send the message "I'm interested in what you're trying to say."

Don't put your kids on the spot. When you say, "Tell your grandma what happened today," you unintentionally put pressure on your child to speak.

Focus on the message. Focus on what your child is trying to say and not on the stuttering.

No teasing! Make this a policy in your home.

Don't ask your child to stop and start over. This increases anxiety instead of alleviating it.

Practice fluency. Let your child practice her speech by repeating phrases back to you.

> ❧ *Many parents worry, "I must have put too much pressure on my child." There is no evidence whatsoever to support the idea that pressure leads to stuttering.*

Take "response-ability."
Ensure that you're connecting with your child in a manner that promotes self-confidence and free communication.

THINK IT THROUGH

Reframe

Ask, "How can I best help my child?"

Reflect

Use the acronym S-T-O-P to clarify your end of the equation.

See. Replay in your mind the situation that is causing you grief._____

_____

Think. How does your thinking influence the situation? ____

_____

Observe. Take a step backward and notice your body language, tone of voice, and facial expressions. _____

_____

Put it together. How do mental and emotional contributions influence your knee-jerk reactions? _____

_____

Resolve

Often a parent blames herself for every difficulty her child encounters. However, respecting your child as a separate person means realizing that you are not at the root of all her problems. This is especially true when it comes to stuttering.

Now, with guilt out of the way, how can you best respond to your child's stuttering?

_____

_____

_____

TEMPER TANTRUMS
What Helps—What Hurts

Sam had a colossal temper tantrum in my office today. One moment he was quietly playing with my equipment while his mother and I talked, and the next moment he was down on the floor kicking, screaming, banging his head, pounding his fists, and pulling down whatever he could grab on top of himself. His mother carried on talking, stopping only long enough to reassure me, "Don't worry, he'll settle down in a moment or two." Toddlers can be completely happy one moment and, with an instant reversal of mood, become irrational and hysterical the next. Many parents (unlike Sam's) react in emotionally charged ways, and outbursts become two-way affairs. This chapter will help you exercise appropriate controls (self-control included) by giving you sanity-saving information and modern advice.

"What Am I Doing Wrong?"

In the heat of the moment, remember this: Tantrums happen because a child can't express or suppress his emotions. They are inevitable. Outbursts disappear as a child's language skills develop, provided a parent doesn't deal with tantrums in a way that reinforces them.

> *MYTH: Tantrums represent bad parenting.*

Although occasional meltdowns are unavoidable, knowing how to minimize and manage them is key. If you can recognize the body language, behavior, and angry expressions that precede a tantrum, you can intervene before things get out of hand. If you have an easygoing child, redirection may be all that's needed to ease her frustration. But if your child is more volatile, you'll need steady nerves, a clear perspective, and a few tricks.

For starters, understanding the innocence of tantrums will allow you to respond to them gently and effectively. A tantrum may seem like a toddler's way of saying "You're a bad mother" or "I'm angry at you." But toddlers lose their temper for entirely different reasons than adults. A tantrum is how a child tells you he's frustrated, hungry, tired, bored, or not coping.

A TODDLER'S TANTRUMS

They Don't Mean	They May Mean
I think you're mean.	I'm really upset.
I don't like you.	I've had enough.
I want to make you angry.	I'm tired.
I'm trying to manipulate you.	I'm frustrated.
I want a new mother.	I'm bored.
I'm bad.	I don't know what I want.

A preverbal child, even a verbal one, talks via her behavior. A youngster doesn't say, "Mommy, I'm bored. I need a change of scenery." She gets antsy, whines, and misbehaves. Tantrums speak volumes. An adult who learns to listen and interpret a preverbal youngster's behavior will help him feel understood and thereby decrease his frustration level.

By no means am I suggesting that you should make excuses for your child's misbehavior or that it should be tolerated because he's tired, hungry, or bored. You need to empathize, not sympathize. Meaning, you need to be supportive but do so without lowering your expectations.

Tantrums will be passionate or mild, frequent or occasional, manipulative or otherwise, depending on how you respond to them. While there is no one-size-fits-all remedy, these strategies will help you defuse and deflect tantrums without rewarding them.

Know when to expect a tantrum. Chances are, you've already noticed that tantrums seem to happen at the most inconvenient times and in the worst possible places. For me, they happen when I'm in a hurry, on the phone, racing against a deadline, in public, or running late. Knowing when to expect a tantrum is highly effective; if it doesn't happen, you'll be pleasantly surprised, and if it does, at least you won't be caught off guard. Think ahead and plan distractions for situations that are not kid-friendly or are likely to be challenging.

Be proactive. When you're going out, think about the environment from your child's perspective and plan accordingly. Jamie, a twenty-nine-year-old stay-at-home mom, always carries a "first-aid kit"—crayons, stickers, gadgets, and favorite snacks in case of an emergency. It never hurts to give your kids a preview about where it is you're going and how you expect them to behave. Focus on dos instead of don'ts: "When we get to the restaurant, I want you to color or play with your Game Boy until dinner is served."

Respond early. Spot distress and step in before things get out of control. My husband and I have a policy to leave outings while the kids are happy. Just like Jerry Seinfeld says, leave on a high note.

Have realistic expectations. Many tantrums are the result of inappropriate demands. Although you may need your child to sit quietly while you talk to the teacher, that doesn't mean your request is realistic. Your expectations need to be age-appropriate and feasible, given the temperament of your child. Come prepared with distractions, and ask yourself, "How can I help my child sit quietly?"

Don't punish. A tantrum shouldn't be rewarded with attention, but neither is it deserving of punishment. How would you feel if you were sent away because you complained about how you were treated at work? You'd feel misunderstood and resentful. We stifle a child's voice when we punish him for expressing himself. What would you need or want in a similar situation? Most likely, you'd want someone who would hear you out and remain calm.

Say what? Although there is no one right way to respond to a tantrum, there are several wrong ways. Here are ways *not* to respond to tantrums:

Don't give in. Giving in to tantrums is one of the easiest mistakes to make. Beware. If you give in often enough, your child may throw tantrums on purpose.

Don't overreact. Losing your temper is normal; after all, you're only human. But if you can control your temper with peers and associates, you can with your kids, too.

Don't fuel tantrums. The only response that doesn't aggravate a tantrum is a firm, clear, and consistent one. Yelling, hitting, bribing, pleading, acting compassionate one moment but angry the next, and yielding are all responses that reward tantrums (remember, kids love positive *and* negative attention) and guarantee problems down the road. You and your child will be greatly comforted knowing that you're in control and able to set boundaries.

Don't hold a grudge. When a tantrum is over, let it be over. Don't talk about it. Don't refer back to it or remind your child about it. Don't dwell on it. Just move on. Holding a grudge nurses anger and leads to more revenge-related tantrums down the road.

For all those tantrums that happen despite your best efforts, the following guidelines will help you respond appropriately.

- *Ride it out*. Without an audience, tantrums are more likely to be short in duration. Your child needs to vent, which is okay, but don't unintentionally reward him by giving too much attention.
- *Get out*. Public tantrums are embarrassing (and inevitable). You know everyone is watching, and you know full well what they're thinking: "My child would never behave like that." And even though a tantrum is not a sign of bad parenting, onlookers will be critical of you. When you handle a tantrum with an audience, you're unlikely to set appropriate boundaries. Leave before a tantrum grabs hold; pick up your child and go somewhere that affords you privacy.
- *Address the problem*. Remember, some tantrums are due to fatigue, overstimulation, boredom, or hunger. If you think one of these is at fault, fix the problem, not the child.
- *Over the top*. Every child is different. An easygoing child will have brief and forgiving tantrums, while an angry or inflexible child may get "stuck" and need you to help him move forward. Some children need to be redirected with a quick hug and reassurance.

Take "response-ability."

I like to tell parents that temper tantrums are like speed bumps—minor obstacles that can't be avoided but can be easily managed. For sure, some toddlers are more tantrum-prone, and some adults will find them more nerve-racking. But no matter what, you will help your child the most by keeping your wits about you. I know this is no small order, but I also know it's something you can do because you're committed to doing your best. Otherwise, you wouldn't be holding this book in your hand.

THINK IT THROUGH

Reframe

Consider: "How do I shape my child's tendency to throw tantrums?"

Reflect

Answer yes or no to the following questions:

I am worried that something is wrong with my child because his tantrums are so extreme. Y or N

Sometimes I give my child what he wants just to avoid a tantrum. Y or N

My child knows full well that public tantrums embarrass me. Y or N

I have a bad temper. Y or N

Tantrums frazzle me. Y or N

I hug my child when he has a tantrum because I believe his behavior reflects unmet needs. Y or N

I believe my child uses tantrums to get his own way. Y or N

I lecture my child about his tantrums. Y or N

I can't go about my business when my child has a tantrum.
Y or N

I cave in too often. Y or N

Score: Add up the "yes" answers.
0–3 You are a pro.
4–6 Tantrums are an issue.
7–10 You are in a rut.

Resolve

Develop a strategy to avoid and respond to tantrums that will ease the situation.

TIP: Remember that tantrums are to a certain extent developmentally inevitable.

I can tell my child is heading toward a meltdown when

_____
_____

When I see this coming, I plan to _____
_____
_____

If I can't avoid a tantrum, I will _____
_____

I need to learn how _____
_____

I suspect my child's tantrums will settle down when I
_____
_____

THUMB SUCKING
Kids Will Give This Approach
Two Thumbs Up

I'll never forget the time I took my daughter Madison, then six, to her first orthodontist appointment. The orthodontist began by speaking to my daughter, not me! I had to bite my tongue to avoid jumping in and answering for her. When I stopped feeling defensive, I began to listen to my daughter's answers. This was one of those defining moments: I realized Madison had her own life that wasn't just an extension of mine. How did I have such a profound experience at the orthodontist's office? When the orthodontist asked Madison if she'd ever tried to stop sucking her thumb, and Madison answered yes, I was dumbfounded. It never occurred to me that Madison had her own feelings about thumb sucking, because I was so caught up with my own.

It turned out that a few months earlier, Madison had tried taping her thumb and fingers together. I remembered the morning when she came down for breakfast with her right hand all taped up. I was annoyed that Madison had wasted so much tape, and I made her take it off before sitting down to eat. I hadn't bothered to ask her why she'd taped up her hand. If I had, I would have discovered that Madison was being teased at school and being called a "baby," and she genuinely wanted to stop sucking her thumb.

Because Madison's thumb sucking was causing her dental problems, the orthodontist gave her two choices: 1) to independently stop sucking her thumb, or 2) to wear a device in her mouth that would make sucking impossible. Madison hated the device, so she decided to break the habit on her own. And the most amazing thing happened after we left the office that day—Madison never sucked her thumb again.

Thumb Sucking—The Facts

Self-soothing. When I went for my prenatal ultrasound, I saw Madison sucking on her thumb in my womb. Sucking is how babies comfort themselves, and it's a natural part of development. Life is full of challenges and stress; although we tend to think of these as adult emotions, babies are bombarded with new experiences each day. Imagine the comfort a child experiences when she is able to soothe herself. When an infant finds her thumb, and sucking on it gives her a sense of relief, she discovers a new level of independence. The problem is, grown-ups have a tendency to interfere. Many parents have a gut-level negative reaction to thumb sucking. I've seen parents come into my office with mittens on their baby's hands, and others who tap the baby's hand and say, "Bad," then pull the thumb out of his mouth. These reactions interfere with a baby's need to suck and deprive him of a powerful self-comforting tool. The most common reason parents give for discouraging thumb sucking is the fear that the baby will suck his thumb when he's older. Usually a parent will go on to tell me how she sucked her own thumb until she was eight, nine, or ten years old.

> *The most common argument I hear in favor of pacifiers is "You can take away a pacifier, but you can't take away a thumb." This is true, but what's not mentioned here is the fact that up to one third of children go on to suck their thumb when the pacifier is taken away.*

The stats. Thumb sucking begins in infancy and most often disappears by middle childhood. According to psychologists, thumb sucking isn't associated with emotional problems, and it isn't a sign that your child is stressed out. Most pediatricians believe that thumb sucking isn't related to the length of time a child is breast-fed. And according to statistics, over 30 percent of kids are sucking their thumbs in the preschool years, while up to 20 percent continue past the age of six.

The issues. There are basically two issues when it comes to thumb sucking beyond six to eight. First, a habitual thumb sucker of this age may end up with buckteeth or other malocclusions. Several orthodontists have reassured me that problems with the front teeth aren't hard to correct; nevertheless, I'd run this by your own dentist, since there seem to be as many opinions as dentists. Second, parents tend to get embarrassed when an older child sucks his thumb, especially in public. Embarrassment for the child may come from peers who will call him a "big baby."

"How Can I Stop My Child from Sucking His Thumb?"

Right after I signed the contract to write this book, my editor paged me. A colleague in her office wanted to know how to get his six-year-old to stop sucking her thumb. I was disappointed not to have a secret cure that would solve his problem and make me look like a hero, but the truth is, you can't force a child to stop a habit (especially one that is a source of comfort and reassurance). The only person who can do this is the child. You can change your own behavior, but you can't force your child to change his. You'll save yourself a great deal of frustration and disappointment if you inspire change instead of demanding it. Let's use our three R's to put this theory into practice.

Take Sarah and Jack, the proud parents of three delightful girls. The youngest, Emily, was a spirited eight-year-old, who sucked on her thumb until it was cracked and bleeding. Sarah and Jack asked me, "Will you tell Emily to stop sucking her thumb? She won't listen to us." I had to help Emily's parents realize that they couldn't bully her into changing her behavior, nor could I. In fact, the more they criticized Emily, the more she needed to suck her thumb to relieve the anxiety created by these fights. As I often tell parents: Pressuring your child to stop sucking her thumb often does more damage to your relationship than sucking does to her teeth.

What could Sarah and Jack do differently that would end the fighting and bring about change? Sarah gave Emily a "You're going to get in big trouble" look when she caught her daughter sucking her thumb. And Jack didn't even realize how much his words stung: "Only babies suck their thumbs. You look ridiculous. Take your thumb out of your mouth." Now, my job as a pediatrician is not to play the heavy—although I'm often asked to do so—but rather to help parents solve their problems. To Sarah and Jack's credit, they became more self-observant and paid closer attention to their end of the equation. Did Emily stop sucking her thumb? Yes, she did—but when she was ready, according to her own agenda. I can't say for sure, but I suspect that Emily would have sucked her thumb even longer had her parents not let up. Clearly, this couple would have been pleased if Emily had stopped sucking her thumb earlier, but they nonetheless appreciated the positive changes in their relationship with her, which they came to see as far more important than the angst they experienced because of her thumb sucking.

Overcoming Thumb Sucking

Collaboration, not coercion. When I realized that my daughter Madison desperately wanted to stop sucking her thumb, I asked her, "How can I help you?" She thought for a moment and said, "Would you remind me to stop sucking my thumb?" We brainstormed and together came up with a few practical ideas on how to keep Madison's hands out of her mouth. What struck me more than anything was the sense of teamwork. Madison learned that she could look to me for support, and I discovered that she was willing to accept my help when she was ready for it. Even if your child doesn't stop sucking her thumb, she'll learn several important lessons; she'll know that she can turn to you with a problem, and that you trust and respect her. But one of the most important lessons she'll learn is this: She is responsible for her own behavior.

Tricks of the trade. What if the dentist or orthodontist says your child needs to stop sucking her thumb? Here are a few tricks that parents have shared with me over the years. No one trick is 100 percent effective—but who knows, maybe one of these strategies will help your child.

- Have your child wear gloves. If she is keen to stop, gloves will serve as a reminder. This is not something I would recommend to deter babies from their hands.
- Use a tensor bandage wrapped around the elbow. This makes sucking difficult from a mechanical point of view, as the child can't bend his elbow to bring his hand to his mouth.
- Bandage the thumb and finger together.
- For girls, try nail polish in a fun color that will serve as a private reminder.

- Try a lollipop that sits on the thumb (available in most candy stores). This is what helped my daughter Madison the most.

Teach, don't preach. Don't assume your child understands why you want him to stop sucking his thumb. Empower him by teaching about his teeth and the effect of thumb sucking on their position and health.

Take "response-ability."

I have to admit that one of my pet peeves is the pacifier. Among other faults, it robs a baby of the opportunity to be independent and comfort himself. Maybe you're wondering if you made the right decision by allowing your child to suck his thumb. But let me ask you, whose thumb is it anyway?

THINK IT THROUGH

Reframe

Ask, "How am I caught up in my child's thumb-sucking habit?"

Reflect

Take a moment and think about the positive and negative ways you and your little one interact around thumb sucking.

_____

_____

_____

_____

_____

Resolve

Approach the problem in a way that assumes you're both on the same team. I plan to

_____

_____

_____

_____

_____

TOILET TRAINING
Succeeding Without Defeating

What are your priorities right now? Do you want to toilet-train your child graciously and peacefully, or do you want to train quickly at any cost? If it's the latter, I suggest you skip this chapter and buy one of those books that teach you how to train your child in less than a day. Otherwise, let me show you how toilet training can unfold naturally and calmly. I guarantee you that your child can learn without fuss, irritation, or even tremendous effort on your part. The key ingredient is respect.

Respect means treating your child as a separate person with her own set of feelings, perceptions, and priorities. How would you feel if someone pressured you to do something you didn't want to do? I suspect you'd be angry and frustrated. Children feel the same way. Parents decide it's time to potty train regardless of whether the child is ready or willing, and they may push twice as hard if the child resists. I don't think parents are intentionally unsympathetic or insensitive. Nevertheless, whether intentional or accidental, the end result is the same: The child feels violated and unimportant.

THE SEVEN THINGS YOU NEED TO KNOW ABOUT POTTY TRAINING

1. Don't train your child before she's emotionally and physically ready.
2. Trust your child, trust the process. Toilet training will become a priority when the child begins to crave independence.

3. Before you begin potty training, your child should be aware when he has a dirty diaper and able to get up and down from the toilet independently. His motor skills need to be good enough that he can scoot around easily and manage dressing without a fuss.

4. If your child resists training, pull back. Don't even mention the potty for weeks unless your child initiates it first.

5. If your child has an accident, be cool and say something like "No big deal. Try again later."

6. There's more to toilet training then developmental and physical readiness. Emotional issues and inner conflicts hold many kids back. You'll save yourself a great deal of frustration if you respect your child's pace.

7. Toilet training shouldn't be done to please you. It's your child's accomplishment, not yours.

> ➤ *The emotional climate around toilet training is the most important ingredient you can contribute to your child's success. Keep an inner dialogue going with yourself on every bump you encounter. Ask yourself: "What am I doing, positively or negatively? What do I need to do differently?"*

The Secret to Successful Toilet Training

Everyone has an opinion about when a child should be toilet trained. Some parents and experts approach potty training like boot camp: The child is put through an intense training program and is expected to be potty trained by the end of a session. On the other extreme are people who believe that a child will train, without adult intervention, when they are physically and emotionally ready. If either of these positions is working for you and your family, then there is no reason to change. But if neither works, don't worry. My commonsense approach is a compromise between these two extremes.

"But My Three-Year-Old Is Still in Diapers"

Let's approach this problem using the three R's. I had one mother, Sheila, whose son was determined to stay in diapers. When I asked her, "Why do you think Tommy refuses to use the potty?," she said, "I'm sure it's because of something I've done wrong." She complained, "Tommy won't even come in the bathroom if the potty is out." I've known many youngsters like Tommy and twice that number of frustrated parents.

The key to solving this problem was to reframe the question. Sheila was focused on all of Tommy's mistakes: "He won't sit on the toilet" or "He poops in his pants" or "He hides in the corner when he needs to poop." By asking instead, "How am I contributing to the situation?," Sheila was able to go to work on the one person she could readily change: herself. A classic stressed-out mom, she was confused by all the conflicting advice she'd gotten from friends, family, the Internet, and her beloved pediatrician. One time she'd be patient and supportive and respond to accidents with "Don't worry, we all make mistakes," and the next time she'd yell, "What's the matter with you?" Sheila went on to explain that she was desperate to toilet-train Tommy because the highly coveted day care she had enrolled him in would not accept him in diapers. This well-meaning mom was not helping things with her inconsistent reactions and not so subtle pressure.

> ⇥ *Don't impose deadlines. Yes, you may need your child to toilet train before he's allowed to attend day care. However, peer pressure works wonders for the physically ready but emotionally "stuck" child. In this situation, I suggest you send your quasi-toilet-trained youngster to day care in underwear instead of diapers, and let him learn from the example of his friends.*

Reflecting on her own behavior helped Sheila understand her responsibility in the overheated potty-training dynamics. This was not a matter of looking at herself as the "cause" of the problem; rather, it clarified what she needed to do differently to reverse negative attitudes. For Sheila, this meant acknowledging and respecting Tommy's resistance and waking up to the fact that he wasn't being difficult on purpose.

The first thing she needed to do was to stop putting pressure on Tommy. He clearly was not prepared to move forward, and his parents needed to listen to what he was trying to say with his behavior. This meant putting away the potty, and although Sheila was terrified to do so, she didn't say a word about diapers, the potty, or day care for a month. Three weeks later, Tommy started to complain when his diaper was wet. He'd go upstairs and take it off, put the wet diaper in the diaper pail, and open up the cupboard to fetch a clean diaper and put it on himself. This was his way of saying, "I don't like being in a wet diaper." It took enormous self-control, but his parents managed to say and do nothing. I suggested to Sheila that she wait a week before asking Tommy if he'd like to use the potty.

"What if he says no?" Sheila asked, obviously dreading the question.

"You say, 'Okay, maybe later,'" I explained, "but even if he says no, leave the potty out and see what happens."

I wanted Sheila and her husband to follow little Tommy's lead, not the other way around. If his parents could maintain a casual attitude, Tommy would show an interest, sooner or later, as does every other child. And when Tommy stopped feeling pressured, he was willing to give the potty a try. His parents praised him when he was successful, and they sympathized with his mistakes. Once they understood they had the power to reshape their problems without strong-arm tactics, they were happier, more confident as parents, and became better advocates for their child.

> ✐ *Once your child has mastered the details of toilet training, your job is to give her the independence that she needs (and wants) by staying out of the bathroom.*

Overcoming Obstacles

Problem

"My child won't even sit on the potty."

Aggravating Factors

You may be putting too much pressure on your child. Frequent reminders may cause her to rebel.

What You Need to Do

Back off. Wait until your child shows an interest before trying again.

•   •   •

Problem

"My little one uses the potty at the sitter's, but she refuses to use it at home."

Aggravating Factors

You child feels conflict about the need to please you.

What You Need to Do

Leave the potty out, but don't urge your child to use it. Avoid comments about being a big girl or boy.

•   •   •

Problem

"My youngster pees on the potty but poops in her pants."

Aggravating Factors

Initially, some children feel uncomfortable with straining while sitting on the toilet.

What You Need to Do

A foot rest will help your child feel secure when he sits at the toilet. Alternatively, you can temporarily offer your child a diaper for bowel movements.

•   •   •

Problem

"My son was toilet trained, but now he's having frequent accidents."

Aggravating Factors

He may be stressed by changes in his life, such as a new baby, a recent move, a new nanny, or a change in family circumstances.

What You Need to Do

If you think stress is the main issue, offer your child a diaper and stay low-key. Otherwise, see your health-care provider to rule out physical problems.

· · ·

Problem

"My son wants to use the potty, but he can't seem to get there on time."

Aggravating Factors

Your child may be ignoring signals that he has to pee because he's too busy playing.

What You Need to Do

Get into a routine. Remind your child to use the potty at the same time every day. Kids love to follow rituals.

· · ·

Problem

"My son knows how to use the potty, but he won't stop asking for a diaper."

Aggravating Factors

Your child may have internal conflicts about the growing-up process.

What You Need to Do

Respect his needs without making any comments like "Big boys don't wear diapers" or "Diapers are for babies." Instead, say, "No problem, here's a diaper."

• • •

Problem

"Since I started toilet training, my son is refusing to have bowel movements."

Aggravating Factors

Constipation is common during toilet training.

What You Need to Do

Be calm. This, too, shall pass. In the meantime, give your child plenty of water and fiber, and an occasional stool softener may be necessary (see "Constipation," page 63).

• • •

Problem

"My mother says I should toilet-train my child by the age of two, but he's not cooperating."

Aggravating Factors

You may be anxious to prove you're a good mother by toilet-training your child "on time."

What You Need to Do

Toilet training happens according to your child's schedule—not yours. Earlier isn't better.

• • •

Problem

"My son wants to pee standing up like his father. What should I do?"

Aggravating Factors

Your child loves his dad.

What You Need to Do

Here's an idea that has helped many little boys: Put food coloring in the toilet bowl, and your youngster now has a target.

• • •

Problem

"My son still wets at night, although he's been dry during the day for years."

Aggravating Factors

There are two opposing theories concerning fluid intake before bedtime:
1. Fluids should be limited before bedtime so the bladder has less to store overnight.
2. Increase fluid intake before bedtime so the brain receives the message loud and clear that the bladder is full.

I suggest you try both approaches and stick with whichever works best.

What You Need to Do

Think of daytime and nighttime training separately. Nighttime training will happen without any effort on your part when your child is physically ready—generally speaking, around three years of age or older (see "Bed-wetting," page 44).

Take "response-ability."

Toddlers communicate through their behavior. When parents listen and observe their youngster's words, actions, and facial expressions, they discover what she needs and are able to respond accordingly. When toilet training is a problem, it means adults aren't hearing what the child is saying. Does a child's resistance to toilet training mean he's stubborn? No, it means he's not ready. Remember, your child is a separate person, and he has his own priorities and feelings about toilet training that must be respected.

THINK IT THROUGH

Reframe

Consider: "How am I contributing to toilet-training dilemmas?"

Reflect

The following questions are designed to help you understand how you are contributing to (not the cause of) potty-training conflicts.

If my child has an accident in her pants, I say, I feel, I think

_____

_____

How do you respond if your child asks for a diaper?

_____

_____

How does your child react when you ask him if he wants to use the potty?

_____

_____

Are you embarrassed that your child is still in diapers?

_____

_____

Why is it important to you that your child is potty trained now?

_____

_____

What would your child say if I asked him how he feels about potty training?

_____

_____

_____

_____

Resolve

Decide on a game plan that is based in respect to deal with conflicts around toilet training.

_____

_____

_____

_____

_____

For each scenario below, fill in how you: a) would typically react, and b) would respond in the best-case scenario.

Your four-year-old asks for a diaper.

a) _____

b) _____

Your three-year-old has an accident a moment after you ask him if he needs to use the potty.

a) _____

b) _____

Your relatives tell you that your son should be toilet trained by now.

a) _____

b) _____

HINT: I urge you to be patient and supportive. Your child is struggling with complex cognitive and emotional issues.

TOUGH TIMES
How to Help Your Kids Cope
When You Can't

What's a tough time? A tough time is when a pet dies, or someone you love is diagnosed with cancer, or when your child is having problems—physical, behavioral, or emotional—and you can't make them go away. A tough time is when your partner tells you he's leaving, you get fired from your job, you have a miscarriage, you get falsely accused of wrongdoing, or someone you love dies. Bad things happen. And when they do, parents are left to cope without coming apart. We don't have the option of going temporarily insane because we have to carry on for the sake of our kids.

Not only that, but we have to help our kids cope when we're barely coping ourselves. A few days ago robbers used a crowbar on my back door and forced their way into my home. No one was hurt. But they stole many items that were precious to me (and of no value to them), like the picture I drew of my grandmother when I was in my artsy phase. They stole my jewelry, they stole my furniture, but more than anything else, they stole my peace of mind. I can't sit here without imagining these awful people running through my house, looting through my drawers, stealing my past, my present, and my future.

But I learned something from this experience. I learned that the more freaked out I was, the more demanding and needy my kids were. I needed space and they needed me. I needed quiet and they needed to talk. I needed change and they needed routine. I needed quiet and they needed activity. How can parents keep the daily routine together on the outside if we're falling to pieces on the inside?

Life is not always happy. Inevitably, we all face difficulties that challenge us. But we grow stronger with each disaster. I've learned how to help my children deal with their fears by learning how to deal with my own. And while I cannot say I am grateful for the pain, I am grateful for the lessons it has taught me. And I've learned that after every loss comes a gain. Of course, each person has her own problems, and each parent has her own solutions. But some generalizations can be made and some direction derived from having managed life's challenges without totally losing it.

Take care of yourself. In an emergency on an airplane, a flight attendant will tell parents to put the oxygen mask on themselves first and then look after their kids. The rationale is that a parent won't be able to help her children if she is unstable herself. The same thing is true with emotional distress. You need to take time and space to heal. You will have more to give to your kids if you give more to yourself.

Be practical. When emotions are raw, even the simple tasks can be enormously demanding. This is the time to focus on only those things that absolutely need to be done. Everything else can wait.

Respect your differences. Men and women handle stress and pain differently. Women need to talk it out, while men "get over it" by working harder and keeping busy. If you misinterpret your partner's coping strategies, you may think he is indifferent or uncaring and feel disappointed and alone; he may need to put his own feelings on hold in order to get through the day. However, when you respect each other's differences, you can help each other survive the difficult times without blame, anger, or hurt.

Positive dialogue. You need to have an open discussion with your child about whatever situation is causing you grief. How and what you tell him will depend on the nature of the problem and your child's age. As a general rule of thumb, it's best to be honest. But that doesn't mean you need to tell your child all the painful details.

Don't create new problems. When Lori's baby died of a heart defect, she found it difficult, even years later, to be firm with her three older kids. As a result, they learned that they didn't need to listen to her, and she has had trouble disciplining them ever since.

Get help. This is the time to allow friends and family to pitch in. Lean on others.

Expect it to take longer. Most of us expect to feel better and get back to ourselves much more quickly than we do. But healing takes time. Don't think, "I should be coping better than I am now." Just believe in the future and hold up in the present.

Find support. Talk with other parents. Find a support group. Speak with others who have dealt with tough times. When I've needed support that wasn't there, I've turned to books.

Why me? When disaster strikes, we all wonder, "Why me?" If you're anything like the other parents I know, you may look for ways to blame yourself. But self-destructive thinking won't help you in the long run. Avoid this line of questioning and instead put your energy into healing.

Fall back on rituals. Routines allow you to function with minimal input or decision making.

Don't make big decisions immediately. The worst time to make a significant decision is when you're overwhelmed. Give yourself time before you make any changes that will have a serious or long-lasting impact.

Don't go there. I don't know about you, but many parents (myself included) worry unnecessarily. I will often worry about things that might happen. When my house was broken into, I worried about what would have happened if one of my kids had been home. I couldn't get this fear out of my mind. I stayed up many nights worrying about all the "what ifs" that never happened but could have. Letting my imagination run wild only increased my anxiety. Don't waste your energy worrying about things that might happen, as this is one sure way to drive yourself and everyone else crazy.

Don't take it out on those you love. I don't know about you, but I'm much more likely to have a disagreement with one of my kids when I'm stressed out or troubled. This adds to my problems, as I end up feeling guilty for taking my angst out on my kids. Treating those you love with kindness will help you heal inside.

It's not easy being a parent when all is not well. But we need our kids more than ever at this time. "When's dinner?" or "Can Jake come over and play?" drags us out of ourselves and into the here and now. Just knowing that you have kids to feed helps you to put one foot in front of the other. And while demands are weights, it's the weights that hold us down and ground us in the present.

TAKE "RESPONSE-ABILITY"

Ask yourself, "How am I dealing with this situation, and what am I teaching my children about coping?" My father taught me a powerful lesson, and I hope to live up to his standards. As I was writing this very chapter, my father was diagnosed with an aggressive cancer. I asked him, "How can you be so calm?" He answered, "I don't want any of you to be scared." My father passed away within a week of our conversation. And that is how he taught me to face adversity with grace. Thanks, Dad.

VOMITING

"Is She Doing It on Purpose?"

Just yesterday I was asked to consult with feisty four-year-old Belinda and her parents because this young girl routinely vomited before going to bed. Apparently if her parents didn't rock her to sleep, she cried until vomiting. By the time I saw Belinda, she was pretty well running the show. Here's how the three R's are helping Belinda's parents work through the problem.

THINK IT THROUGH

Reframe

Ask, "How am I contributing to my daughter's bedtime problems?"

Reflect

Use the acronym S-T-O-P to help you zero in on your behavior.

See. Replay the situation that is causing you grief. "I indulge Belinda to avoid a scene."

Think. How does your thinking influence the way you respond? "I think, 'I can't upset Belinda or she'll get sick.'"

Observe. Take a step backward and notice your body language, tone of voice, and facial expressions. "I'm

---

frowning and a little rough in my handling, because Belinda's too heavy for me to rock to sleep."

Put it together. Understand your emotional and mental contribution to the problem. "I'm angry with Belinda for manipulating me. And I'm angry with myself for allowing Belinda to manipulate me."

Resolve

Belinda vomits when she's upset because she has a very sensitive gag reflex. Her parents realized that they needed to set firm limits, and react as calmly as possible, if and when Belinda vomits. This would send the message that vomiting is neither a good nor a bad thing.

Eventually, the parents learned to ward off vomiting by distracting Belinda: "I can see you're getting upset. Why don't we read a book?"

WEANING
How to Wean Without Being Mean

Even though I am a baby expert by profession, and I breast-fed and survived sore nipples, leaking, and biting (four times over), I would never presume to tell another mother when to wean her baby. This is an entirely personal decision, although just about everyone seems to have a strong opinion on the matter. After scouring the Internet, I am impressed by the not so subtle pressure put on mothers contemplating this issue; no wonder so many need reassurance about their decision. That's where I come in.

WEANING MYTHS

When I was a pediatric resident, I was taught that a mother should bind her breasts to help dry up her milk supply. However, as a mother and a physician, I have found that it's a great deal easier and less painful not to. Instead, I recommend that you pump your milk, but just enough to relieve the pressure. Your body will soon get the message to produce less milk.

I have learned to think about weaning in terms of both the baby's needs and the mother's needs. In my experience, weaning is not a decision that a mother makes on a whim, and I for one would not question it. To do so would be akin to a parent telling me how to practice medicine. But what if you're less certain—what are you to do? Try to think about what will be best for both you and the baby, then decide what's right for your situation. Gather information from reliable sources, think about your options, and ultimately, trust yourself; you know what's best.

> *Making a mother's needs a priority is important to me, since every other message she receives in her role as a new mother tells her otherwise.*

Introducing a Bottle

Breast to Bottle.
Going back to work is the most common reason for mothers to wean or to introduce a bottle. Many babies resist the change, which can be stressful for both mother and baby. One way to avoid weaning problems is by giving an occasional bottle once the baby is well established on the breast. You can introduce a bottle without worrying about nipple confusion once the baby is gaining nicely. Do this before the baby is two or three months old, and you'll save yourself a great deal of grief. Many parents I know (myself included) wait until a month or two before returning to work to introduce the bottle. When the baby resists, they buy every nipple and formula on the market, hoping one will do the trick. But there are no tricks. Here are some commonsense strategies to try when introducing the bottle is turning out to be a challenge.

- Have someone else give the baby the bottle.
- Offer breast milk in the bottle.
- Try varying the temperature of the nipple by running it under hot or cold water.
- Try a preemie nipple.

- Don't keep trying different nipples, as this leads to confusion.

Weaning from the Bottle

Bottle to Cup.
Weaning is a process that can take place gradually or rapidly, depending on the temperament of your child. There are two basic approaches: One is to gradually reduce the amount of milk in the bottle until the youngster loses interest, and the other is to just do away with the bottle—literally throw it out, end of story. I can almost hear some of you gasping, but it's easier for some children to adjust and adapt when they know there is no room for negotiation.

Have a positive attitude. When we think of weaning, we tend to focus on the loss of the bottle. But what about the accomplishment involved in using a cup? Little ones learning how to drink from a cup—which means a switch from sucking to sipping—is an accomplishment worthy of attention. Take your child shopping and let her pick out a cup. Then put her favorite drink in the cup and offer it to her with meals. Your child will find using a cup more attractive if she perceives that you value this accomplishment.

Bye-bye bottle. In my experience, somewhere between eighteen months and two years is a relatively pain-free time to eliminate the bottle. If you're going to gradually wean your child, put less and less milk in the bottle. Don't get into a fight with your child about whether or not she can have the bottle; just gradually decrease the servings. If at all possible, plan to keep your child busy when you begin weaning, because many kids ask for bottles out of boredom. In this situation, avoid saying yes or no and simply distract your child with an activity or out-ing. Eventually, you will be able to discard the bottle without making yourself or your child miserable.

> *Allowing your child to take a bottle to bed puts him at risk for dental caries and ear infections. If your child needs a bottle to fall asleep, than you have more reasons (not fewer) to wean.*

Some babies find the weaning process highly stressful. In this situation, it is often best to wean the child quickly in order to avoid prolonging the process. I have used this approach with my own four children and with many youngsters in my office. My husband and I actually bought a cupcake and put a candle in it to make a celebration of saying good-bye to the bottles. As always, I assumed my kids had the inner strength they need to deal with these transitions, and I kept telling them that in the first few days when they asked for their bottle. I'd say, "I know you want your bottle. But you're a strong child, and I know you can deal with saying good-bye to it."

Encourage a transitional object. Your little one is losing a crucial self-comforting tool and has not yet discovered new ways to soothe himself. That's a problem. It's reasonable to encourage an attachment to a "lovey"—a blanket, pillow, or stuffed animal—before beginning the weaning process.

The biggest mistake. Many parents call me and say, "Dr. Cathryn, my three-year-old won't give up the bottle." This is one of those times when you've missed the window of opportunity; you can't expect weaning to happen without initiation and reinforcement by you. A three-year-old is not going to willingly give up the bottle, so it's up to parents to help him. Expect your child to cry for the bottle, and be prepared to deal with this situation without caving in. You'll find it easier to manage if you believe in your child's ability to handle the frustration that weaning entails.

One thing at a time. Don't try to wean your child from the bottle (or breast) and the pacifier simultaneously. Many of the principles we discussed for the bottle apply to the pacifier. You can make limitations on when and where your child uses a pacifier, and you can keep increasing these limitations as the child develops other ways to comfort herself. Some children find this process stressful and are better off getting it over with all at once.

> ❧ *Just yesterday I was asked to see a four-year-old regarding obesity. It turned out the young girl was still on a bottle and consuming an enormous quantity of milk each day. I helped the mother by teaching her how to wean her youngster, and I reassured her that her daughter would naturally drink less milk. Problem solved.*

Bedtime bottles. Breaking this habit takes tremendous resolve, but drinking a bottle in bed leads to dental caries and ear infections. You're the best judge of which approach is best for your child. Never underestimate her; most children make the transition more easily and more quickly than parents anticipate.

Take "response-ability."

The older the child, the less willing he'll be to give up his bottle. Parents often say, "He refuses to give up the bottle." But the real problem here is the adult. You need to believe in your ability to comfort your child, and have confidence in your child's ability to comfort himself. Use the three R's to ensure that you have a positive influence on the situation, and to discover how to best support your child.

THINK IT THROUGH

Reframe

When difficulties arise, ask yourself, "How am I enabling weaning problems?"

Reflect

Every child is different, as is every parent-child relationship. Describe the difficulties you're experiencing around weaning.

_____

_____

Now describe it from your child's perspective.

_____

_____

Resolve

How can you help your baby make the transition from breast to bottle or bottle to cup?

_____

_____

RED ALERT: The older the child and the greater the attachment, the bigger the loss and the harder it is to wean.

WHINING
Defuse with Dignity

As we headed off on our family vacation, a ten-hour drive, I was looking forward to using the unclaimed time to get a head start on my next chapter. However, after defending myself against my daughter Madison's whining from Toronto to New Jersey, I realized that I desperately needed to get a handle on this issue before we headed back home in two weeks. In all fairness to Madison (who wasn't feeling 100 percent that day), she wasn't deliberately whining to get on my nerves, but having hit on something effective, she just wouldn't let up. To make matters worse, once the other kids saw how well whining was working for her, in no time at all, they were all kvetching about one thing or another: "Marissa won't share her music." "Max ate all the crackers." "Why can't we stop?" "How much longer?" The turning point came after I realized how I was reinforcing misbehavior. In this chapter, I'll discuss the philosophies and tools you need to end whining wars. While I can't guarantee that your child will stop altogether, I am confident that these tips will minimize whining significantly. At the very least, you'll be able to deal with whining in a levelheaded and reassuring manner.

The Parents' End of the Equation

Whining is a strategy a child uses to get her way. That's not to say she doesn't whine for other reasons, but whining is a powerful tool that a child uses to manipulate others. For instance, you may be dead set against buying your youngster an ice cream before dinner, but you cave in because your five-year-old is whining, "D-a-d-d-y, can I have an ice cream? Why can't I have an ice cream? You let Jill have an ice cream last week." It's been a long day and you don't have the energy to fight. So you end up saying, "Okay, but the next time you ask for a treat before dinner, the answer is no—so don't bother asking." A few nights later, as you drive by the ice-cream parlor, your youngster again asks, "Can I have an ice cream? You let me have one last time." Again you say yes to avoid a fight. There are many ineffective ways to respond to whining, and knowing what doesn't work is as valuable as knowing what does. Here are some examples of ineffective reactions.

"Do as you're told." In this dogmatic approach, a parent uses fear and intimidation to coerce a child to behave. In his view, a child should learn to respect authority and listen to her parents without needing to be told twice. He's worried that she'll grow up to be a brat unless he lays down the law. But the problem is that when a parent reacts strongly to whining, it causes the child to feel powerful, and this in turn makes whining highly attractive.

"Do you understand why the answer is no?" A parent who is wishy-washy may go to great lengths to explain why she is taking a particular stand. In reality, she may be hoping the child will back down so she can stop feeling guilty about saying no.

"Maybe next time—okay?" This is a typical mistake that many parents make. When parents ask a kid's permission to say no, they are guaranteed an argument.

"Oh, all right." This parent hates seeing her child upset. She may roll her eyes and start off using threatening tones, but she caves in because her child's whining makes her feel like a "bad" parent.

"Would you please stop whining?" This is the reaction I'd expect from a parent who is likely to give in due to exhaustion.

> ❧ *When kids whine, it makes parents feel guilty,
> desperate, frustrated, and powerless. The sooner the
> whining ends, the sooner we feel better about
> ourselves. Parents give in to put an end to whining
> but also to make these feelings of inadequacy go away.*

"Okay, you don't have to go to your skating lesson." This parent feels helpless because her daughter is putting herself down about not being a good skater. Here, the child is directing the parent.

> ❧ *Children whine to get their way, to feel powerful,
> or because they are tired, bored, hungry, or
> stressed. Each problem has a different solution. So,
> take a moment to think about why your child is
> whining before you respond to it.*

The Three R's

Sally, a thirty-two-year-old toy-store owner in Toronto whose three-year-old daughter I've looked after since birth, was desperate to put an end to her youngster's whining. Whenever sweet Rachel cried, Sally would feel frustrated and cave in. At every office visit I'd say to Sally, "You need to be firm and stop feeling guilty about saying no to Rachel." But when Rachel whined, Sally felt miserable.

I was able to help Sally using the three R's. I asked Sally to think about the question "Why do I keep caving in to my child's whining?" This is a far more effective question than "Why won't Rachel stop whining?" By changing her focus, Sally felt a wave of relief—no longer was she trying to change her daughter. Through reflecting on her own behavior, Sally realized that she had a tendency to submit to Rachel's demands. The consequence of her action was that Rachel had learned to whine to get her way. But her mother did not want to raise a whiner. To change the dynamic, Sally needed to assume responsibility for her end of things, because as she had learned, her behavior maintained and shaped her daughter's, and vice versa.

The next day, when Rachel whined that she wanted to eat her dinner in front of the television, Sally said, *"No."* Rachel complained, "All my friends get to watch their favorite programs and eat, so why can't I?" Sally felt guilty, and her impulse was to retract her decision, but she was 100 percent determined to handle things differently. "I felt awful," Sally recalled, "but I knew that being firm was in Rachel's best interest." Sally knew her guilt feelings were powerful and that she needed more than good intentions to keep her from caving in, especially if she was stressed out or tired. She needed a plan. She decided that she would count to ten in her head before answering Rachel's whining, and she'd use these few seconds to calm herself down. She tested out this strategy a few times and found that ten seconds was way too long; she needed to hold back only a few seconds. But then what? Learning to change her behavior was like learning a whole new language. What would she say when Rachel whined? Sally came up with a few one-liners and used them as needed. Now, rather than putting her energy into trying to change her daughter, she uses it to change her way of handling things. Here's another example:

"Mom—why do I need a bath?" asked little Rachel.

"Because your hair's dirty," Sally answered.

"Can't I have a bath tomorrow?"

Sally repeated, "It's time for your bath."

"Why can't I have a bath tomorrow?" asked Rachel.

Sally thought about what she was going to say and decided she didn't need to give an explanation. Instead, she said, "What color bubble bath do you want?"

"I don't want any," grumbled Rachel. In the past, Rachel's pouting was a surefire way to make her mom back down. Sally thought, "Sure, I feel bad that Rachel's upset, but that's my problem."

By then Rachel was getting into the tub, wearing her "oh poor me" face, and was refusing to play with her toys. Her mom thought, "Okay, I feel miserable. But I can handle it." She said to her daughter, "Sweetheart, you have to have a bath. But you don't have to enjoy it."

Take "response-ability."

When you see whining according to the fifty-fifty formula, you realize that part of the problem belongs to the whiner and the other to the person on the receiving end. Both the whining and the reaction to it cocreate the problem. By getting real about your contribution, you become empowered. No longer do you need to try and change your child. Instead, you discover that you can reshape the problem by going to work on yourself.

THINK IT THROUGH

Reframe

Begin by asking yourself, "How am I contributing to my child's tendency to whine?"

Reflect

What am I doing to give my child the impression that whining is effective?

_____

_____

_____

What is the payoff for whining from your child's perspective?

_____

_____

_____

What is the payoff for you in how you respond to whining?

_____

_____

_____

Resolve

What can I do differently that will send the message that whining will not work?

_____

_____

_____

Better yet, how can I use whining to teach my child to be up front, not uppity, about her needs?

_____

_____

_____

HINT: Remember to think in terms of changing your approach, not changing your child.

SOME FINAL WORDS

Trust me, there will always be problems. Good ones, bad ones, and everything in between. They may be harder to remedy than you think, take longer to mend than you expect, and seem more frustrating than you ever imagined. But please, never give up hope or stop trying. You now have the tools and philosophies you need to resolve them. Use what you've learned to empower yourself to bring out the best in your child, and I guarantee you—your child will bring out the best in you right back!

RESOURCES

Every problem has a solution and every solution is within your reach

ANGER

When Kids Are Mad, Not Bad: A Guide to Recognizing and Handling Your Child's Anger, by Henry Paul, M.D., Berkley Publishing 1999
   This book serves as a guide to managing and understanding a child's anger.

Hot Stuff to Help Kids Chill Out: The Anger Management Book, by Jerry Wilde, Lgr Productions 1997
   Child psychologist Jerry Wilde speaks to kids about how to manage their anger as opposed to being controlled by it.

Don't Rant and Rave on Wednesdays! The Anger-Control Book, by Adolf Moser, Landmark 1994
   A book designed for older children to help reduce anger and manage behavior.

The Dance of Anger, by Harriet Lerner, HarperCollins 1997
   Dr. Lerner teaches women how to use their anger to make positive changes in their lives and relationships.

ASSESS YOUR PARENTING PROBLEM-SOLVING STYLE

Team Spirited Parenting, by Darlene Powell-Hopson and Derek S. Hopson, John Wiley and Sons 2001
   A book about how parents can work together to raise well-adjusted and well-behaved kids.

I Only Say This Because I Love You, by Deborah Tannen, Random House 2001
   Linguist Deborah Tannen clarifies why talking to family members is often complicated by the history of our relationships, and teaches us how to improve our communication.

BACK TALK

Backtalk: Four Steps to Ending Rude Behavior in Your Kids, by Audrey Ricker, Ph.D., and Carolyn Crowder, Ph.D., Simon & Schuster 1998
  The authors teach parents a four-step strategy on how to respond rather than react to back talk.

BED-WETTING

www.bedwetting-nkfonline.org
  The National Kidney Foundation provides bed-wetting information.

The National Kidney Foundation
1-888-WAKE-DRY (9253-379) U.S. only
  Advice on treatment options.

BICKERING

Siblings Without Rivalry: How to Help Your Children Live Together So You Can Too, by Adele Faber and Elaine Mazlich, Avon Books 1998
  This book guides parents on how to create peaceful sibling relationships with humor, compassion, and understanding.

Preventing Sibling Rivalry: Six Strategies to Build a Jealousy-Free Home by Sybil Hart, Ph.D.
  Practical steps you can take to promote strong and loving connections.

Beyond Sibling Rivalry: How to Help Your Child Become Cooperative, Caring, and Compassionate, by Peter Goldenthal, Owl Books 2000
  This is a thoughtful book on ways to ease family relationships, based on understanding a child's needs.

www.sikids.com/sportsparents/psychology
Sports Illustrated for Kids
  An insightful review of how to handle sibling rivalry in sports.

BITING

No Fighting, No Biting, by Else Homelund Minarik and Maurice Sendak (illustrator), Harper Trophy 1978
  Age 4–8: A charming story about two alligators who are like two little children.

CONSTIPATION

When You've Got to Go!, by Janelle Kreigman, Spotlight 2000

Age 4–8: Written to teach children about listening to their body when it's time to use the potty.

CRYING

101 Ways to Soothe a Crying Baby, by Jim Peinkofer, Contemporary Books 2000
    A lovely book for new parents, especially parents of colicky babies.

365 Ways to Calm Your Crying Baby, by Julian Orenstein, M.D., Adams Media 1997
    A book designed to calm parents and babies, or at the very least make you laugh.

Why Is My Baby Crying?: The Seven-Minute Program for Soothing the Fussy Baby, by Bruce Taubman, White Hat Communication 2000
    An easy-to-follow plan that will help you understand your baby's cries and respond appropriately.

Secrets of the Baby Whisperer, by Tracy Hogg and Melinda Blau, Ballantine Books 2001
    How to read and understand a baby's nonverbal communication and respond accordingly.

DISCIPLINE DILEMMAS

Secrets of Discipline: Twelve Keys for Raising Responsible Children, by Ronald Morrish, Hushion House 1998
    An intelligent and commonsense approach to discipline.

How to Behave So Your Children Will, Too!, by Sal Severe, Ph.D., Viking Press 2000
    This book teaches parents how to change their behavior rather than focusing on what kids are doing wrong.

The National Parent Information Network
www.npin.org/links
    Offers extensive and reliable links on children's health and development links.

Parentsoup
www.parentsoup.com
    A comprehensive general parenting site.

Parents' Place
www.parentsplace.com
    Another excellent site for parents.

www.canadian-health-network.com
Health information you can trust.

The American Academy of Pediatrics
www.aap.org
Offers policy statements and research-based studies on health, development, and behavioral issues.

The Canadian Pediatric Society
www.cps.ca
A reliable source for solid up-to-date information.

Medscape
www.medscape.com
A medical information and education site for health professionals.

www.generalpediatrics.com
The general pediatrician's view of the Internet is a good source for solid evidence-based research.

DIVORCE

www.divorceasfriends.com
A former divorce lawyer teaches parents how to divorce as friends and maybe save the marriage.

www.divorcesupport.com
This website is devoted to connecting adults to the most valuable and comprehensive divorce-related information.

www.divorcecentral.com
Divorce central offers help, support, and information.

www.divorcemagazine.com
A divorce magazine for Generation X.

Helping Your Kids Cope with Divorce the Sandcastle Way, by M. Gary Neuman, Random House 1999
An empathetic and essential guide on how to divorce without hurting your children. Please read this book!

Parenting After Divorce: A Guide to Resolving Conflict and Meeting Your Child's Needs, by Philip Stahl, Impact Publishers 2000
Dr. Stahl helps parents avoid the routine mistakes divorcing couples make

and understand the impact of the divorce on the children; he also guides parents on how to best settle their differences to avoid hurtful consequences for children.

Parents Without Partners
401 N. Michigan Avenue
Chicago, IL 60611-6267
312-644-6610
www.gocrc.com
  A nonprofit organization devoted to the welfare of single parents and their children.

Children's Rights Council
220 I Street N.E.
Suite 230
Washington, D.C. 20002-4362
www.gocrc.com
202-547-6227
  The CRC is dedicated to the rights of children who are members of a divorced family.

EMOTIONAL VITAMINS

Children Learn What They Live, by Dorothy Law Nolte, Workman Publishing 1998
  A set of inspiring principles for instilling positive values.

FEARS

Keys to Parenting Your Anxious Child, by Katharina Manassis, M.D., Barron's 1996
  Expert advice on how to understand and respond to your child's anxiety.,

Some Things Are Scary, by Florence Heide and Jules Feiffer (illustrator), Candlewick 2000
  Age 3 and up: Faces children's fears in a creative and reassuring manner.

FOUL LANGUAGE

The Berenstain Bears and the Big Blooper, by Stan Berenstain, Random House 2000
  Age 4–8: How Mama Bear deals with foul language at the dinner table.

HEAD BANGING

I'm Frustrated (Dealing with Feelings), by Elizabeth Crary, Parenting
Press 1992
> *Age 4–8: A book that teaches kids different ways to handle their frustration.*

HIGH-MAINTENANCE (SPIRITED) BABIES AND KIDS

*Raising Your Spirited Child: A Guide for Parents Whose Child Is More Intense,
Sensitive, Perceptive, Persistent, and Energetic,* by Mary Kurcinka,
HarperPerennial Library 1992
> *This book offers parents proven strategies and support for raising a "difficult"
> child.*

INTERRUPTING

How to Talk So Kids Will Listen and Listen So Kids Will Talk, by Adele
Faber and Elaine Mazlich, Avon Books 1999
> *The authors teach parents how to communicate with their kids and make rela-
> tionships at home less stressful and more meaningful.*

INTRODUCING THE NEW BABY

Loving Each One Best: A Caring and Practical Approach to Raising Siblings, by
Nancy Samalin, Bantam Books 1997
> *A guide to surviving the pitfalls and experiencing the rewards of parenting
> two, three, or more children.*

And Baby Makes Four: Welcoming a Second Child into the Family, by Hilory
Wagner, Avon Books 1998
> *This book guides parents through the complications and challenges affecting a
> growing family.*

Big Kids Preparation Classes
> *Most hospitals and birthing centers provide classes for siblings. Contact your
> local hospital for further information. On the Internet, there are extensive list-
> ings of individual and private organizations that provide classes. Enter
> "Sibling Preparation Classes" into any search engine.*

JEALOUSY

Preventing Sibling Rivalry: Six Strategies to Build a Jealousy-Free Home, by
Sybil Hart, Free Press 2001
> *This book teaches you strategies to create a jealousy-free home.*

KVETCHING

Feeling Thankful, by Shelley Rotner, Millbrook Press 2000
Age 4–7: A photo essay that guides kids on recognizing and appreciating the good things in their lives.

The Thank You Book for Kids: Hundreds of Creative, Cool, and Clever Ways to Say Thank You!, by Ali Lauren Spizman, Longstreet Press 2001
Age 9–12

LIES, FIBS, DECEPTIONS

10-Minute Life Lessons for Kids: Fifty-two Fun and Simple Games and Activities to Teach Your Kids Trust, Honesty, Love, and Other Important Values, by Jamie Miller, HarperPerennial Library 1998
Teaches positive principles through games and activities.

LISTENING

What Did I Just Say?: How New Insights into Childhood Thinking Can Help You Communicate More Effectively with Your Child, by Deborah McIntyre and Denis Donovan, Owl Books 2000
The authors teach parents how to communicate more effectively and improve relationships with their children.

Setting Limits: How to Raise Responsible, Independent Children by Providing Clear Boundaries, by Robert J. Mackenzie, Prima Publishing 1998
How to set sensible limits without using strong-arm tactics.

Tired of Yelling: Teaching Our Children to Resolve Conflict, by Lyndon D. Waugh, M.D., Pocket Books 2000
Renowned family psychiatrist Lyndon W. Waugh provides solutions for more peaceful living.

MEDICINE DISPENSERS

www.babiesrus.com
Ingenious medicine dispensers are available on-line.

MESSY BEDROOMS

Organizing from the Inside Out, by Julie Morgenstern, Owl Books 1998
How to overcome obstacles and get organized. This book will help adults get a handle on their own messes and, in so doing, be able to set a good example for their kids.

Max Cleans Up, by Rosemary Wells, Viking Children's Books 2000
Age 4–8: A fun book that will leave you smiling and a little more sensitive about kids and the mess they leave behind.

Simplify Your Life with Kids, by Elaine St. James, Andrews McMeel 1997
A book about how to simplify one or two areas of your life in order to improve the quality of your time and relationships at home.

NIGHTMARES AND NIGHT TERRORS

The Monster Bed, by Jeanne Willis, Mulberry Books 1999
Age 4–8: This story is about a monster who is afraid of humans. It's a fun book about bedtime fears.

Monsters in Your Bed . . . Monsters in Your Head, by Rainey Freidman, Dream Dog 2000
Age 4–8: A children's picture book that helps kids to overcome bedtime fears.

OVERWEIGHT KIDS AND UNDERLYING ISSUES

www.kidshealth.org
Excellent information on children's health and well-being from the NeMours Foundation.

Fat-Proof Your Child, by Joseph Piscatella, Workman Publishing 1997
A balanced approach to diet and exercise with practical solutions that will help you and your kids get in shape.

American Academy of Pediatrics Guide to Your Child's Nutrition, by William H. Deitz, Villard Books 1999
A state-of-the-art guide to children's nutrition and eating habits.

PICKY EATERS

D.W. The Picky Eater, by Marc Tolon Brown, Little Brown & Co. 1995
Age 4–8: A picture book about picky eating that will make you laugh.

I Will Never Not Ever Eat a Tomato, by Lauren Child, Candlewick Press 2000
Age 3–8: A children's book that infuses levity into food battles.

Eat Your Peas, by Kes Grey, DK Publishing 2000
Age 4–8: A battle of wills ends in a comical standoff.

POUTING

Let's Talk About Needing Attention, by Joy W. Berry, Scholastic 1996
  Age baby to preschooler: A story about how a youngster learns positive ways to get attention and the differences between good and bad attention.

POWER STRUGGLES

Kids, Parents, and Power Struggles, by Mary Sheedy Kurcinka, Quill 2001
  The author teaches parents how to avoid struggles and connect with their child.

Try and Make Me!, by Ray Levy, Ph.D., and Bill O'Hanlon, Rodale Press 2001
  A commonsense approach to handling parenting problems that involves seven steps to changing difficult behavior and attitudes.

QUARRELS

Raising Respectful Kids in a Rude World: Teaching Your Children the Power of Mutual Respect and Consideration, by Gary McKay, Ph.D., Prima Publishing 2001
  Teaches parents how to restore common courtesy and respect in families.

SCHOOL PROBLEMS YOU MAY ENCOUNTER

www.chadd.org
  Children and Adults with Attention Deficit Hyperactivity Disorder (CHADD) official site.

www.ldanatl.org
  The Learning Disability Association of America is a nonprofit organization dedicated to advancing the educational and general welfare of children and adults with learning disabilities.

Normal Children Have Problems, Too, by Stan Turecki, Bantam Doubleday 1995
  Helps parents understand and deal with a child's emotional problems.

Playground Politics, by Stanley Greenspan, M.D., Perseus Press 1994
  Gives parents a greater understanding of a child's mind and heart from kindergarten on.

Dreamers, Discoverers, and Dynamos: How to Help the Child Who Is Bright, Bored, and Having Problems in School, by Lucy Jo Palladino, Ballantine Books, 1999

> *Psychologist Lucy Jo Palladino identifies what she calls the Edison Trait—children that are precocious of mind and spirit but do poorly in our educational system.*

Going to School: How to Help Your Child Succeed, by Sharon Ramney and Craig Ramney, Goddard Press 1999

> *The comprehensive book on how to prepare your child for school and how to best support him.*

SCHOOL REFUSAL

Benjamin Comes Back, by Amy Brandt, Red Leaf Press 2000

> *Age 4–8: A comforting story about coping with separation anxiety.*

SHARING

Mine!, by Kevin Luthardt, Atheneum 2000

> *Age 4–8: A picture book about sharing.*

Me, Myself, and I: How Children Build Their Sense of Self, Eighteen to Thirty-six Months, by Kyle Pruett, M.D., Goddard Press 1999

> *Dr. Preutt helps parents understand the development of a child's personality and how to best guide her to become her finest self.*

SHOPPING DISCIPLINE

It Worked for Me!, by *Parents Magazine* (editor), Griffin Trade 2001

> *A collection of tried-and-true ideas and solutions from parents across the U.S.*

SHYNESS

The Shy Child: Helping Children Triumph over Shyness, by Ward K. Swallow, Ph.D., Warner Books 2000

> *A guide for parents of shy children.*

How Kids Make Friends: Secrets for Making Lots of Friends, No Matter How Shy You Are, by Lonnie Michelle, Freedom Publishing 1997

> *Age 6 and up: An informative and fun guide to help children make friends.*

Buster: The Very Shy Dog, by Lisze Bechtold, Houghton Mifflin 1999

> *Age 4–8: How Buster overcomes shyness and discovers his self-worth and self-confidence.*

SKINNY KIDS

American Academy of Pediatrics Guide to Your Child's Nutrition, by William H. Deitz, Villard Books 1999
> *A state-of-the-art guide to children's nutrition and eating habits.*

SLEEP ISSUES

The National Sleep Foundation
www.sleepfoundation.com
> *A nonprofit organization committed to improving public awareness of the importance of sleep.*

Sleeping Through the Night: How Infants, Toddlers, and Their Parents Can Get a Good Night's Sleep, by Jodi A. Mandell, Ph.D., HarperCollins 1997
> *A child psychologist offers practical tips on bedtime and a straightforward approach for improving sleep habits.*

Healthy Sleep Habits, Happy Child, by Marc Weissbuth, M.D., Fawcett Books 1999
> *A distinguished pediatrician offers a detailed regime to ensure good sleep habits.*

Sleeping Like a Baby, by Avi Sadeh, Yale University 2001
> *Dr. Sadeh suggests a wide variety of practical solutions to babies and young children's sleep problems. This book is unique in acknowledging that there is no one-size-fits-all solution.*

Solve Your Child's Sleep Problems, by Richard Ferber, Simon & Schuster 1986
> *A practical guide to common sleep problems for children ages one to six, based on Dr. Ferber's research as the director of Boston's Center for Pediatric Sleep Disorders at Children's Hospital.*

SPOILING AND UNSPOILING

How to Say No Without Feeling Guilty, by Patti Breitman, Broadway Books 2001
> *The book that will help you set limits with your children and in your own life.*

SPORTS AND PARENTS

Parent Association for Youth Sports (PAYS)
1-800-688-KIDS

This organization is dedicated to educating and motivating sports parents to make a child's sports experience safe and meaningful.

www.momsteam.com
This site is a resource for moms about youth sports.

www.nays.org
This organization helps parents and youth leagues work together to provide the best sports experience for kids.

www.positivecoach.org
This organization guides parents on how to provide a favorable playing experience for kids.

STUTTERING

Solid advice for parents of a child who stutters.

The National Stuttering Association
www.nsa.org

The Stuttering Foundation of America
www.stuttersfa.com

The National Center for Stuttering
www.stuttering.com

The American Speech-Language-Hearing Association
www.asha.org

The National Stutterer's Hotline (U.S. and Canada)
1-800-221-2483

The American Speech-Language-Hearing Association
1-800-638-8255

Ben Has Something to Say: A Story About Stuttering, by Laurie Lears,
Albert Whitman & Co 2000
Age 4–8: This book helps kids who stutter to know they are not alone.

TEMPER TANTRUMS

The Chocolate-Covered-Cookie Tantrum, by Deborah Blumenthal, Clarion
Books 1999
Age baby to preschool: A picture book that demonstrates a youngster's strong emotions.

THUMB SUCKING

American Academy of Pediatric Dentistry
www.aapd.org

The American Academy of Orthodontists
401 North Lindbergh Boulevard
St. Louis, MO 63141
314-993-1700

TOILET TRAINING

Potty Time, by Guido van Genecten, Simon & Schuster 2001
Age baby to preschool: A gender-neutral book that focuses on the emotions that a toddler may experience while learning to use a potty.

Parenting Guide to Toilet Training, by Anne Krueger and *Parenting Magazine* (editor), Ballantine Books 2001
A relaxed, effective approach to toilet training from Parenting Magazine.

TOUGH TIMES

When Children Grieve, Leslie Landon Matthew, Ph.D., HarperCollins 2001
A manual to help children deal with death, divorce, pet loss, moving, and other sources of distress.

VOMITING

Easy to Love, Difficult to Discipline, by Beck A. Bailey, Ph.D., William Morrow & Co 2000
A powerful approach to solving behavioral problems.

WEANING

How Weaning Happens, by Diane Bengson, La Leche League International 2000
A guide to weaning with love.

WHINING

Whining: Three Steps to Stopping It Before the Tears and Tantrums Start, by Audrey Ricker and Carolyn Crowder, Fireside March 2000
A straightforward guide to end whining.

INDEX

Academic problems, 213–214
Acceptance
  of children, 94, 146
  of partner's views, 27
Accidental parenting, 18, 25
Adaptability, 118
Aggression, 30, 212
American Academy of Pediatrics,
  77, 249
Anger, 30–37
  expressing, 30
  five ways not to respond to, 31
  reacting to, 34–35
  Reframe, Reflect, Resolve, 36–37
  resources, 327
  support groups for, 32
Antidiuretic hormone (ADH), 44,
  46, 47
Anxiety, 212
Anxiety disorders, distinguishing
  between fears and, 102–103
Asthma medications, 211
Attention deficit disorder, 211
Attention problems, 214
Authoritative parenting, 18, 24
Autonomy-versus-independence
  issues, 39

Back talk, 38–43
  overcoming, 40–41
  Reframe, Reflect, Resolve, 42–43
  resources, 328
  responding to, 39–40
Bad language, 106–110
Balanced meals, myth of, 240

Bargaining, 270
Bath, fear of, 98
Bathroom habits, 65, 66
Bathroom talk, 106
Bed-alarm system, 46, 47
Bedrooms, messy, 166–169
Bedtime bottles, 264, 317, 318
Bedtime rituals, 248, 259–261
Bed-wetting, 44–49, 304–305
  after dryness, 47–48
  attitude toward, 45–46
  doctor's role and, 45, 46
  practical steps, 44
  Reframe, Reflect, Resolve, 48–49
  resources, 328
  statistics on, 46
Behavioral problems, at school,
  210–211
Bickering, 50–58
  boredom and, 53
  jealousy and, 54
  Reframe, Reflect, Resolve, 55–58
  resources, 328
Birch, Herbert, 117
Biting, 59–62
  dealing with, 59–61
  reasons for, 59
  Reframe, Reflect, Resolve, 62
  resources, 328
  treating bites, 61
Blended families, 270
Blood, in stool, 64
Boredom
  bickering and, 53
  eating and, 180

ABOUT THE AUTHOR

Cathryn Tobin, B.I.S., M.D., F.R.C.P.(C), has devoted her entire adult life to working with families. Besides being the mother of four, she has worked as a general and consulting pediatrician in Ontario, Canada, for more than a decade. Prior to that she trained and practiced as a midwife in the United States and Canada.

She currently lives in Toronto with her husband and four children, who inspire her, time and again, with problem-solving opportunities.